Praise for *Cap in Hand*

"I've always believed that being a philanthropist involves more than simple charity. To me, the most effective philanthropy is about addressing root causes of problems, about empowerment, justice and social change. I have worked side-by-side with Gail Picco as we sought to bring about change in Regent Park, Canada's oldest public housing project, a project that today leads the world in inner city transformation. Now Gail has written a book that draws a comprehensive picture of charity in Canada and around the world. The book zeros in on charity vs. social change, treatment vs. prevention and handouts vs. empowerment. It shows us what we can do to positively impact the lives of millions of people around the world. This is important work. All I can say is, "Brava!""
—Mitchell Cohen, President & CEO, The Daniels Corporation

"Gail Picco has worked with many international NGOs and brings a nuanced and powerful critique to the table. I have worked with her and know her well. From a deeply ingrained sense of activism, she is courageous, boundary pushing, inquiring and willing to challenge conventional thinking. This book is brave, searching and necessary. It comes at the right time, from the right place, for all the right reasons."
—Nicole Salmon, Boundless Philanthropy

"Since her earliest days as an activist, Gail Picco has consistently dug deep to understand the roots of injustice. She's challenged us to be discontented with snipping at the offshoots of evil and to, instead, focus on eradicating its roots. In this courageous and timely book, Gail dares to challenge the charitable sector to dig deep and evaluate its objectives and measures of success."
—Denny Young, Program Coordinator and Professor, Fundraising Management Program, Humber College

Also by Gail Picco

What the Enemy Thinks: A Beck Carnell Novel

Cap in Hand

How Charities are Failing
the People of Canada and the World

Gail Picco

civil sector press

Cap in Hand: How Charities are Failing the People of Canada and the World

ISBN: 978-1-927375-41-9

Library and Archives Canada Cataloguing in Publication

Picco, Gail, 1959-, author

Cap in hand: how charities are failing the people of Canada and the world / Gail Picco.
Includes bibliographical references and index.
Issued in print and electronic formats.
ISBN 978-1-927375-41-9 (softcover).--ISBN 978-1-927375-42-6 (Kindle).--
ISBN 978-1-927375-43-3 (EPUB)

1. Charities. 2. Fund raising. I. Title.
HV41.2.P52 2017   361.7   C2016-908130-3   C2016-908131-1

Cap in Hand: How Charities are Failing the People of Canada and the World

Published by Civil Sector Press, Box 86, Station C, Toronto, Ontario, M6J 3M7 Canada
Telephone: 416.345.9403
www.charityinfo.ca
Publisher: Jim Hilborn
Edited by: Lisa MacDonald
Cover and book design: Cranberryink

To

Rambunctious instigators
Intrepid animators
Reasoned castigators
Fearless initiators

Love makers
Booty shakers
And ball breakers

All over the world.

This book is for you.

Ill fares the land, to hastening ills a prey,
Where wealth accumulates, and men decay.
— Oliver Goldsmith (1730-1774)

Contents

Preface

In July 1973, the *Toronto Star's* Sidney Katz heralded the opening of one of North America's first shelters for battered women with the headline, "*The rising wave of runaway wives — Women are liberating themselves: they say to heck with it and leave.*"

Nine years later, in 1982, I was hired as a counselor at that shelter.

In an effort to pin the tail on the patriarchal donkey, we counselors, whose job descriptions made all of us chief cooks and bottle washers, spoke to journalists and columnists like Sidney Katz. We said yes to television reporters who wanted to come by the shelter for a quick stand-up interview to talk about the causes of violence against women or respond to breaking news like the response to Farrah Fawcett's 1984 film, *The Burning Bed*, the O.J. Simpson trial or news of a previously anonymous man killing his wife.

We buttonholed elected politicians at every opportunity. Armed with statistics, anecdotal evidence and analysis, we did speech after speech, meeting after meeting with social workers, police officers, lawyers, church groups and lawmakers, wanting them to understand and take action on violence against women. We viewed ourselves as advocates.

We knew that providing shelter and support to women fleeing violence without trying to deal with the system that allowed such violence to persist did not make sense.

But we had other worries, particularly about money. The shelter was always full. The length of our waiting list was a howling reminder of the services that were needed. We were going to have to become good at something most women would rather eat nails than do. We were going to have to learn how to ask people for money.

The thought was not appealing, but eventually we got our heads around it.

Weren't people who gave us money just an extension of our movement? Not everyone could be on the front line with us, but some could help by writing cheques and we'd heard that if you mailed a letter to 5,000 people or more, Canada Post would give you a break on the postage. At a time when the term "cheque book activism" was used somewhat derisively to denote people who were not really committed, we embraced it and began to recruit supporters using direct mail. Direct marketing was our ticket and we jumped in with both feet, penning clear and emotional letters to caring people (who showed they were caring because they had given to another charity) telling the stories of the women who came to us for help.

Soon we were measuring our daily mail by the inch. Hundreds, then thousands, of people sent in large numbers of small donations. Far from making us feel beholden, our fundraising tool made us independent and powerful. How democratic!

But eventually eight years of working at the shelter took its toll on me. After my first child was born, the thin film of membrane that separated my own psyche from the psyche of the women and children at the shelter had evaporated. The hurt they felt, I absorbed. It had all became too close, too hard. The time had come for me to move on.

Yet during my time at the shelter, I had learned a great deal about fundraising and the impact it could have on people's lives. I was convinced of its usefulness and started a fundraising and communications consulting company, which ended up, over the next 20 years, having some of the country's most interesting nonprofit groups as its clients.

But what I didn't quite realize at the time is that I had made a leap from activism to charity, a chasm I never fully appreciated until the jump had been made. And, in the intervening years, as activism of the kind that brought attention to issues like violence against women has retreated, that crevasse has widened execrably.

There's the parable about two men fishing alongside a riverbank when a crying, drowning baby floats by. The men swim out to the baby and bring her safely to shore. Just as they get to the riverbank, they see two more crying, drowning babies floating by. As soon as they reach the riverbank with those infants, they see another two crying, drowning babies floating by. One man dives straight back into the river and the other runs away, upstream. The man in the river calls out, "Hey Joe, where are you going? Aren't you going to help me with these babies?" "I'm going upstream to see why these babies are ending up in the river," Joe replies and runs off.

Having spent 25 years working in, and observing, the charitable sector, I understand that charities in Canada and around the world have done a better job at grabbing babies out of the river than running up the river to find out why the babies are there in the first place.

My hope in writing *Cap in Hand* is that once charities better understand the forces at play throughout the sector and how charities intersect with public policy as a whole, they will realize how much power they have to facilitate real solutions to some of the world's most intransigent problems.

So much more can be done. Right now. This day.

Instead of devoting so much talent and resources to figuring out better ways of plucking crying, drowning babies from the water, charities have it in them — with some externalized analysis and accountability, reflection and institutional courage — to become agents of long-lasting change so that someday there will be *no* crying, drowning babies in that river.

If charities take on the mantle of *transforming* the systems that make people sick, sad, marginalized and poor — and are supported by their donors in doing that work — I am convinced that it is within our grasp to turn charity into change: positive change that will impact untold millions of people in our country and around the world.

But let's begin by drawing a picture of this thing called the charitable sector.

Introduction

The amount of money generated by charities from private-sector fundraising in Canada and around the world has never been greater than it is today. In certain sectors, the sums of cash are unprecedented.

Toronto's Princess Margaret Cancer Hospital's current *Believe It!* campaign for personalized cancer treatment research has a goal of $1 billion. When University of Toronto unveiled its $2 billion *Boundless* campaign, the largest fundraising campaign in Canadian history, on November 20, 2011, it ripped that top spot right out of the hands of west coast university, UBC, which 43 days previously had made its own historic $1.5 billion declaration for its *Start an Evolution* campaign.

You could be forgiven for thinking the timing a cold-blooded move that, while personifying the competition in the sector, no doubt contributed to the numerous reasons why many Canadians hate Toronto.

The amounts of money in play are particularly mind-boggling in consideration of results.

- Has the quality of post-secondary education improved as a result of massive investments of private cash to Canadian universities where first year courses routinely have classes numbering in the hundreds or even thousands of students?

- Do indigenous people living in remote communities have clean drinking water because of the endowed research chairs at universities and hospitals?
- Has cancer been beaten? Why not?

How are the hundreds of millions of dollars raised every year for bio-medical cancer research rationalized while medical authorities the world over are telling us prevention initiatives will save *more* lives? Why do we give to charities? How do they ignite our passion? Defy our logic?

In the past two decades, as fundraising has become the raucous tail wagging the accommodating dog, charities have lost sight of their missions. Many do not judge their success on their progress in ending poverty, curing cancer or whatever the purpose of their existence, but on how much money they raise and how little they spend on administration.

Trust in charities is diminishing and manipulation by charities is growing as they spend more money to develop new ways of marketing to people's most intimate fears.

In the past 20 years, we've watched the gap between the rich and the poor grow. Unsurprisingly, that equity gap is mirrored in the charitable sector. Wealthy charities, with the resources to dominate every marketing channel, effectively take in an ever-increasing percentage of the oxygen, leaving less well-off organizations with scarcely the ability to breathe.

But charities are not obliged to care about the *common* good. Their constituency is the people who are related to *their* mission, the people underneath *their* umbrella. They don't have to concern themselves with people under other umbrellas or with people with no umbrella at all.

In order to declare success, the charities, generally speaking, don't need to concern themselves with the cause of global issues such as climate change, refugees, inequity and the growing incidences of cancer and other chronic disease. Most feel their job is well done if they keep the money and the clients flowing through their organization in equal measure, without rocking the boat.

Their attention and resources is on the person sitting across the room from them, which is, very often, a donor.

In this book, I share interviews with cancer researchers, international development workers, hospital foundation chieftains and people who have been observing charities for decades. Their observations and experiences make up the story I want to tell you; a story I think is important for you to hear. It is a story that will take you behind the lemonade stand, the fundraising gala and that brand new hospital wing.

I will be telling you where charitable dollars go, who controls the spending and how decisions are made. Some of it might surprise you.

1/

The Sight of the Forest

There are 33 pages of legislation regulating the production and marketing of maple syrup in Canada.

After a decade of research, negotiations and the garnering of feedback from consumers and the industry, and based on recommendations from the International Maple Syrup Institute (IMSI), a common maple syrup grading standard for Canada and the United States was unveiled through amendments to the Canadian *Maple Product Regulations Act* in 2014.

According to the Canadian Food Inspection Agency, the new standards introduce flavour descriptors that will help consumers make more informed choices when buying maple syrup…descriptors that will categorize pure maple syrup on a scale ranging from "Golden Maple Syrup with a delicate taste" to "very Dark Maple Syrup with a strong taste."

Canadian Senator, Nancy Greene, a beloved Olympian skier who won gold at the 1968 games in Grenoble, France weighed in on the subject when the new regulations were unveiled.

"Not only will these amendments provide maple producers greater freedom to market their products internationally," she said, "they will make it easier for Canadian consumers to purchase the syrup they prefer. The new grades and colour classes will help Canadians make more informed choices when shopping for our high quality maple syrup."

Nancy Greene dominated the sport of skiing when she was active during the sixties and seventies. She is now 72-years-old and it seems like she would know as well as anyone what she was talking about on the very Canadian matter of maple syrup.

Canada is responsible for 84 per cent of the world's maple syrup production. Canadian exports of maple syrup exceeded CAD $145 million (approximately USD $130.5 million) last year. The United

States kicked in a plucky 16 per cent of world output, mostly from the state of Vermont.

And although hipsters are winning the day in some quarters and maple syrup is losing cachet as an international hostess gift (what exactly does one *do* with it?), Canadians continue to take their maple syrup seriously.

In 2011, the country couldn't turn away from news of a brazen robbery coming out of Saint-Louis-de-Blandford, Quebec. In what amounted to the biggest maple syrup heist in history, a ring of thieves stole 16,000 barrels of the world's back-up supply of maple syrup, known as the Global Strategic Reserve, held in case of a bad sap year, just by trucking it out of the warehouse and re-filling the barrels with water. The syrup wasn't guarded or even locked up because people couldn't imagine anyone wanting to steal it. But the thieves understood the market. They saw that every barrel in that warehouse was worth more than 30 times the price of a barrel of oil which, at the time, averaged USD $110. They built up a network of drivers, rented warehouse space and made the necessary industry connections to fence six million pounds of contraband. And it was just sitting there for the taking. Only one quarter of it was ever recovered.

There's a lot more than meets the eye in the land of maple syrup.

And just like maple syrup, our perception of charities, the topic of this book, can be pretty sweet. But, similarly, what's going on underneath that feel-good taste is all business. What looks straightforward on the surface can be far more nuanced and complex when that surface is scratched.

The story of charities, in Canada and the Western world, is nothing if not complex.

Charity's provenance is scriptural. In the Christian Catholic tradition, for example, charity is one of the seven heavenly virtues that, along with prudence, justice, temperance, courage, faith and hope can form a path to true happiness. In that tradition, charity means love. Love in the sense of an "unlimited loving kindness towards all others." It is held to be the ultimate perfection of the human spirit, because it is said to "both glorify and reflect the nature of God."

Charity is necessary for salvation, Christian teachings allow, and with it you can take comfort that you will never be spiritually lost. However, the teachings specify, it should not be confused with the "more restricted modern use of the word charity to mean benevolent giving."

We can probably consider the barn door closed on the interpretation of charity as a path to the "perfection of the human spirit."

Here on this mortal coil, we have given in to our confusion and unequivocally embraced the concept of "charity as equal to benevolent giving." When thoughts of charity occur, if they occur at all, they are most likely to be triggered by a child holding a box of cookies in her outstretched hand or the subject line of a friend's email declaring he is "riding for a cure."

The result is the same. We dig into our pockets.

And all that digging has turned charity into a world of big business and big money.

It's a big pie.

In Canada, charities generated $246 billion of revenue from all sources in 2014, an amount of money that situates the sector between the number 43 country of Ireland and the number 44 country of Pakistan on the World Bank's GDP Rankings of 195 countries. The charitable sector in Canada employs more than two and a half million people in full and part-time positions, second only to the retail sector. It is currently sitting on $373 billion of assets including cash, investment funds, endowment funds and real estate. Each year, cash rich charities invest in everything from national bonds to foreign currency to hedge funds.

It's a similar story throughout the industrialized world. Although harmonized data is impossible to come by, we do know that in 2013 U.S. charities generated USD $1.73 trillion of revenue and were sitting on USD $3.22 trillion of assets. U.K. charities generated £64 billion in revenue and were holding £142 billion in assets.

In 2014, the first year the figures became available in that country, AUD $103 billion of revenue flowed through Australian charities as they held onto AUD $202.9 billion in assets.

And because charity mirrors the society in which it operates, the top one per cent of charities is holding onto ninety-nine percent of the charity pie.

In Canada, there are *ten* pages of legislation regulating the registration of charities.

2/

Following the Money

For the past decade Mark Blumberg has been on a mission.

The Toronto-based lawyer understands the dynamics of charity in Canada and around the world as well as anyone. He had been working in it and observing it for a decade and a half. He works at a small law firm that has nine lawyers, five of whom focus on nonprofits and charities. He has a Bachelor of Laws from the University of British Columbia and a Masters of Laws from Osgoode Hall Law School in Tax Law.

He is the editor of www.canadiancharitylaw.ca, a charity law website, and www.globalphilanthropy.ca, a website dedicated to supplying news about the charitable sector as well as information on legal and ethical issues for Canadian charities operating in Canada or abroad. He offers charity law "boot camps."

Information about charities pours out of him like an uncorked bottle of brandy.

As he grabs examples of what he's trying to explain from history, the front page of the newspaper and his own experience, his words sound as though they are running to keep up with his thoughts, even while he throws in the occasional stream of consciousness joke to keep the mood high. The result is beguiling, the listener charmed into thinking that there surely could not be anything more interesting in that moment than charity law.

Mark's devotion to charity transparency stands out because media reporting on the sector, beyond the occasional scandal or feel good story, is thin. Evaluative techniques within charities, if they exist at all, are often focused on internal operations as opposed to external impact.

The general perception of charities is that they are neighbourly endeavours, but not really much of a factor in the fate of nations.

But in a sector not used to empirical attention, Mark has done everything but shake us by the shoulders saying, "come on, there's this huge thing called the charitable sector over here and no one is paying attention."

One of Mark's megaphones is *Blumberg's Snapshot of the Canadian Charity Sector.*

He summarizes information from the Canadian Revenue Agency data on Canada's 85,000 charitable organizations from hospital foundations and universities to food banks and international relief organizations and releases it as a *Snapshot.*

"Every person—it doesn't matter if you work with five charities, one hundred charities or three hundred charities—forms their perception of the sector based on the charities he or she has worked with," says Mark.

The idea of the snapshot is to draw a picture of the *entire* sector he says. Like any good lawyer, Mark also says we have to understand there are always provisos whenever he posts his snapshot statistics. However, the statistics he generates from Canada Revenue Agency (CRA) data gives us a picture of where the sector is at today and gathering up-to-date information plays a vital role in increased understanding of the sector.

"The big shock to me," says Mark, "and I've been doing this since 2004, is not that I'm doing it, it's wondering why others are *not* doing it?"

Canada is in a better position than most countries to understand what is going on in charities because all Canadian charities are obliged to file a tax return and because everything on the charity's tax return, the T3010 form, is put into one database and can therefore be used for analysis. The form is about the same length as a personal tax return and collects basic information about a charity's operation in its fiscal year.

To *not* file your T3010 is to put your charitable status in jeopardy. One Canadian organization, Charity Intelligence, mostly comprised of investment analysts who have assumed a mandate to evaluate Canadian charities, awkwardly had its charitable status revoked in 2012 for not filing their T3010. The organization wiped the egg off its face, filed the necessary forms, applied for and had its charitable status re-instated, and got on with the business of rating charities within six months.

The *Blumberg Snapshot of the Canadian Charity Sector 2014* has recently been released and one of the most remarkable insights, aside from the actual size of the sector, is how much government money runs through the charity "system."

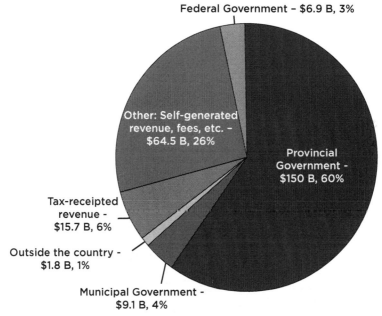

Figure 2.1: Revenue highlights from Blumberg's *Snapshot of the Charity Sector, 2014.*

The sector generated $246 billion in total revenue on $228 billion in total expenditures in 2014.

More than 65 per cent of the money spent by charities comes from government and 26 per cent comes from self-generated revenue including fees. Canadian charities are holding onto $373.1 billion in assets; $15.7 billion in official donation receipts were issued by charities.

Yet the majority of charities are small and volunteer run—52 per cent reported having no employment expense at all.

Mark's transparency work has played a significant role in defining his professional life, but his continued work on transparency also has a deeply personal angle. The snapshots are a part of the *Sean Blumberg Transparency Project,* named after Mark's brother who had been integrally involved in the gathering of statistical information on Canadian charities for the Blumberg Snapshots and other articles.

For fifteen years, Sean suffered from severe depression and paranoia. Mark says he was kind and gentle; the project was very meaningful to him and this voluntary work offered him a vital interest. Although Sean had access to the best doctors and ongoing loving support from his family, things became increasingly difficult for him to bear. When Sean took his own life four years ago, Mark decided to name the transparency project after him, continuing to put up material that is free and accessible.

"I find it interesting," he says, "when people talk about the size of the charitable sector in Canada, the number $110 billion is often referenced because they are using numbers from eight or ten years ago when the last big national voluntary sector study was conducted. The size of the sector now is over $240 billion. So, what's the point of talking about $110 billion from ten years ago?"

—·—

The United States has 1.4 million charitable or 502(c) 3 type groups. Data is collected through the filing of their 990 forms. The Internal Revenue Service (IRS) has recently made electronically filed Form 990s available in a digitally sortable format, but still some religious organizations in the U.S., such as the Salvation Army or the Church of Scientology, are exempt from filing annual 990 forms. And other single donor foundations, such as The Bill and Melinda Gates Foundation fill in a different form, so straight country comparison is not possible.

In other countries, only PDF copies of an individual charity's tax return are available online. That is adequate if you are looking for information on one charity, but impossible to use if you're looking for sector-wide data. For that you need the information in a digitalized format so that you can sort from top to bottom, to find out which charities have the most revenue, expenditures, assets or who is spending on political activities, whatever it is you want to know.

Here is what we can compare for the value of the charitable sector in Canada, the U.S., the U.K. and Australia.

	Canada (CAD)	U.K. (GBP)	U.S. (USD)	Australia (AUD)
Number of charities reporting	84,521	163,709	954,476	54,223
Assets	$373.1 billion	£142.08 billion	$3.22 trillion	$202.49 billion
Annual revenue	$246 billion	£64.41 billion	$1.73 trillion	$103 billion
Tax-receipted donations/ voluntary income	$15.7 billion	£18.10 billion	$358.38 billion	$6.8 billion
Charitable revenue as a per cent of a charity's total revenue	6.16%	28.80%	13.30%	6.60%
Population	35.5 million	64.1 million	316.5 million	23.1 million
Amount donated per capita	$441.71	£267.71	$1,061.81	$293.99

Figure 2.2: Charity by country comparison.

In the Western world, charitable organizations are a primary way governments deliver health and social services.

In addition to funding from provincial tax bases, in Canada the federal government funnels money to the provinces through federal transfer payments, which fall into four categories. The health transfer payments fund hospitals and healthcare. Social transfer payments fund post-secondary institutions, social services and childcare. Equalization payments, the third category, re-distribute revenue so provincial capacity is equalized. The fourth form of transfer payments, Territorial Formula Financing, is basically designed to do the same thing as equalization payments, but are applied to Canada's territories—the Northwest Territory, Yukon and Nunavut.

The *Canada Health Act* obliges provinces to provide a health-care system that upholds the pillars of universality, accessibility and portability. In 2014, federal transfer payments and funding from provincial tax bases provided $150 billion to charities to deliver health care and social services.

And although the $15.7 billion of tax-receipted donations in 2014 is an exceedingly sizeable sum in anyone's books, those charitable donations supplied only 6 per cent of the charitable sector's annual revenue in that year.

That is not to say revenue from donations is not important to charities or to addressing social issues.

Individual citizens can have a tremendous role in determining the issues we want our governments and societies to address. It cannot be underestimated. In a democracy, making a donation can be another way of casting a ballot. It is a donor, a citizen, a voter saying, "this is what is important to me, and I'm prepared to put my money into it."

HIV/AIDS and breast cancer are two issues eventually brought into the mainstream of medical research and government funding through the actions of citizens.

In 1984, for example, the fear of AIDS was so thick that media crews refused to enter offices of the newly formed AIDS Project Los Angeles (APLA) to cover the story and charitable foundations declined to meet with APLA representatives afraid of being infected with the deadly virus.

Enter Elizabeth Taylor.

The reigning monarch of Hollywood royalty was prepared to press her every, not insignificant, advantage to raise awareness of AIDS.

In the earliest days of the outbreak, she hosted the first-ever AIDS fundraiser, an event called *Commitment to Life* in support APLA bringing together some of the biggest names in the entertainment industry including Carol Burnett, Sammy Davis, Jr., Burt Lancaster, Cyndi Lauper, Shirley Maclaine, Burt Reynolds and Rod Stewart.

Taylor raised $1.3 million that evening, the equivalent of $3.0 million today. And while the significant and effective street protests organized by the AIDS Coalition to Unleash Power (ACT UP) were still a few years away, the revolution needed to conquer AIDS had begun.

In what must have been a great source of motivation for her, but also a source of great sadness, was that while she was planning the APLA event, she learned that her longtime friend, Rock Hudson, was dying of the disease.

Similarly, while it might be hard to recognize it as such now, creating awareness about breast cancer was also once a movement of the people.

Breast cancer, a primarily woman's cancer occurring in a sexualized part of the body, was considered somewhat shameful. To speak the word breast in public was risqué. Women's health in general, but diseases involving the reproductive system in particular, were not discussed. We don't have to go very far back in history to hear women talking about their health concerns being marginalized.

The initial uncloaking of breast cancer as a women's issue was brought to light by affected groups of women working at a grassroots level.

Charlotte Haley is one example. She was featured in the 2011 National Film Board of Canada's documentary, *Pink Ribbons, Inc.* and was one of many women across North America working at a grassroots level to bring more attention to breast cancer. Her grand-mother, sister and daughter had all suffered from the disease.

In 1992, disturbed by the lack of resources going into aware-ness and research of breast cancer, she made little peach-coloured ribbons and attached them to cards that read, "The National Cancer Institute's annual budget is \$1.8 billion, only 5 per cent goes for cancer prevention. Help us wake up legislators and America by wearing this ribbon."

Charlotte distributed the ribbon and call-to-action cards at the supermarket, and sent them to high profile people including the wives of U.S. presidents and Dear Abby.

Eventually, Evelyn Lauder, senior vice president of the cosmet-ics company Estée Lauder, noticed Charlotte's grassroots campaign and peach ribbon. She wanted the cosmetics company to join the growing cadre of ribbon-wearers promoting social causes, a trend that originated in the United States to acknowledge wars vets that was immortalized in the 1973 pop hit, *Tie a Yellow Ribbon Around the Old Oak Tree* by Tony Orlando and Dawn.

Charlotte Haley was approached to do a deal with Estée Lauder for Breast Cancer Awareness month but she didn't think it a good fit. It was too corporate and too commercial for her taste. She refused. Estée Lauder went ahead without Charlotte's peach ribbon. They simply changed the colour to pink, "the quintessential female color." And that kicked off a series of events, which has brought us to the pink ribbon world we live in today, a world that bears little vestige of the grassroots movement that originally put the issue on the map. Charlotte Haley passed away in 2014 at the age of 91.

—-—

Charitable donations can be especially effective in solving social problems if charities leverage their public support to unlock other avenues of funding and involve themselves in confronting root causes, devoting at least part of their resources to see why all those crying, drowning babies are in the river in the first place.

The HIV/AIDS movement personifies this ideal. It is a movement that began in an environment almost entirely obscured by stigma and bias; a time when a government worker reportedly burned the dress she was wearing after handling a piece of paper that had been touched by an AIDS patient. That was only 1984. Yet, the movement—powered by money and activism, and led by the gay community—drove social change to a point where the disease's epidemiology is now, by and large, accepted and understood. And to where, with the advent of anti-retroviral drugs, an AIDS diagnosis no longer means a death sentence—all in the span of 25 years.

Government entices us to be better than our best selves by incentivizing charitable donations through a system of tax credits. The more money you give, the better the tax break you get. From a charity's perspective a dollar is a dollar is a dollar, whether the donation is from a spiritually self-actualized philanthropist, a grudging giver or a wily businessman with an eye to the bottom line.

The symbolic value of the $15.7 billion given in gifts to charity is more than its face value. Of that there is no question. But if we want to analyze the charitable sector *as a whole*, government is by far the biggest player. Yet, with shifting political winds, government funding can be precarious.

And it is this precariousness that worries Mark Blumberg, especially the 60 per cent of the sector's total worth in Canada—or $150 billion—that is coming from federal transfer payments and provincial governments.

"If government were to cut back money going to charities, that is, potentially, hugely impactful," says Mark. "If provincial governmental funding where to be cut by just 10 per cent or $15 billion, which is very doable…many countries are seeing much bigger cuts right now …fundraising revenue would have to *double* what they currently raise to make up that deficit in government funding."

By comparison, American charities get a lot less in government funding, making them much more reliant on individual donations. But there's a danger in that position too. In 2008, because of the recession, American charities saw a 10 per cent decrease in charitable donations. In 2009, they faced another 15 per cent decline in donations. In two years, they lost approximately a quarter of the annual amount generated by charitable donations.

"Now, if we went down 25 per cent in terms of our giving, here in Canada, at $15 billion," Mark says, "you're be talking about losing three or four billion, right? There, you're talking about a much bigger amount."

In fact, American charitable giving shrank by more than $80 billion in the 24 months of 2008 and 2009. In 2013, total private giving from individuals, foundations, and businesses totaled $335.2 billion, and although total charitable giving had risen for the fourth consecutive year, it was still lower than its pre-recession peak of $348.0 billion in 2007. The Urban Institute's Center for Nonprofits and Philanthropy in Washington, D.C., which analyzes trends in American nonprofits, referred to the recession as delivering the "triple whammy" of reduced government funding, a decline in charitable donations and increased need.

News of charity bankruptcies and closures filled U.S. media outlets from the *Wall Street Journal* to the *Huffington Post*. Well-regarded regional charities in the U.S. had to shut their doors and many more cut staff and reduced services.

"It was apocalyptic what happened there," says Mark. "And some people in Canada were talking as if we were going through the same thing as the Americans were going through. But we didn't have a decline in donations at all. In Canada, donations over that time *increased*."

———

Judging a charity's effectiveness is a tough job.

The idea that a good charity doesn't spend any more than 15 per cent on administration has gained great favour in the past decade. But that criterion can be quickly debunked if you compare the amount of due diligence, preparation and process that's required to work in a conflict-ridden war zone to what's needed in order to gather up and distribute food for an urban food bank. One requires a tremendous amount of work that's defined as administration. The other does not.

Low fundraising costs are another benchmark used to rate a quality charity. But that's not really quite fair either. Because organizations who have a small number of large donors (including government) are going to have much lower fundraising costs than an organization that depends on a large number of small donations, which are significantly more expensive to solicit and process. Yet the organization that survives on small donations is arguably more democratic and accountable to its constituency.

Beyond that, what else is being discussed about the efficacy of charity?

Donors sometimes bring questions to the table that help a charity to articulate its relevance, but some donors, especially donors who give large amounts of money, often come to the table with their own agenda, an agenda that is often quite unrelated to how well a charity executes its mission in the broader context of good public policy.

The reporting on government funding is not particularly helpful in judging effectiveness either.

"With government funding, there is often a large amount of paperwork that must be submitted on a monthly or quarterly or annual basis. But most of this material is not made available to the public. Nor does it seem to be analyzed or acted upon or used in any significant way," says Mark Blumberg.

An Auditor General oversees government spending, but when the Auditor General is reporting on an issue, it's more about the government's failure than the charity's failure.

"Some people tell me 'we're not worried so much about money that's coming from government because they can take care of themselves, they're big boys,'" says Mark Blumberg. "I don't view it that way. I think the easier approach is to try to have accountability across the board. It doesn't matter if they get it from one donor, from government, from individuals or from business enterprises. In the end, we want all of them to be accountable."

If the charitable sector is tough to evaluate, it's also difficult to regulate.

Charitable organizations run the gamut. Some are volunteer-driven outfits with budgets of $35,000, no employees and no assets. If we were only talking about a sector with groups like that, you could make an argument that we need a simpler system or maybe we don't need any regulation at all. But charities also include large institutions with 5,000 employees, annual budgets of $750 million and a billion dollars in assets.

Yet the same rules apply to all charities regardless of size. These rules were designed more to encourage good works and altruism than to monitor investments, disbursement quotas and asset allocation.

"It's just like our society," says Mark Blumberg. "You have the 99.9 per cent who have something and you have the .1 per cent—it's not even the 1 per cent—who have a heck of a lot more. But a lot of the complaining I see is the .1 per cent feeling they don't have enough flexibility to do what they want to do."

Despite the fact that charities are the main deliverer of the country's social and health services, as revenue of $246 billion can attest, the volunteer leadership of most charities struggle with how to do their jobs well.

Volunteer board members, whose qualification for the job is often simply their desire to "give back," may or may not have any experience in the nonprofit sector or in the specialization of the charity's mission.

There are no courses volunteer board members need to take or minimum criteria they need to meet. Yet, they arrive at the charity in a position to wield the ultimate power over its activities. They determine policy, hire and fire CEOs and pass or reject the charity's budgets. The oversight for the management of the sector's $246 billion in annual revenue and $373.1 billion in assets in Canada, as well as its success in fulfilling its mission, rests in the hands of volunteers with no training and, in most cases, no prior experience in the nonprofit sector.

What could possibly go wrong?

Journalism and a free media has been viewed throughout the history of democracy as an elemental part of its functioning.

Edmund Burke—the 18th century oratorically-blessed Irish-born Anglican who served in the British House of Parliament and viewed by some as a father of modern conservatism—has been attributed with coining the phrase "the fourth estate" to describe the media *in toto*.

"There were Three Estates in Parliament, but, in the Reporters' Gallery yonder, there sat a Fourth Estate more important far than they all," Burke said in 1787 in a speech to support the press's coverage of parliamentary proceedings.

The three other estates referenced by Burke included the Lords Spiritual (bishops of the Church of England), the Lords Temporal (non-bishop members of the House of Lords) and the House of Commons.

Whether in a 18th century British parliament or a 21st century frenzied free-for-all, media is understood to be, in a democracy, part of the circle of accountability between political bodies, public institutions and the citizenry. Without accurate and "objective" information about how our institutions operate and what they are doing, the citizenry cannot even begin to make knowledgeable assessment.

A free and inquiring media is not only required for a democracy to thrive, it is necessary for society's institutions to perform in society's best interests and to be held accountable.

And nowhere is the media more absent than in their coverage of the charitable sector—which remains seated, after decades of trillions in spending and arguably questionable results—with pursed-lipped stoicism behind a shimmering veil of goodwill.

Somehow, journalists who courageously pose questions to war-mongering tyrants often hold back from a thorough investigation of the charitable sector.

When Canada's national newspaper, the *Globe and Mail*, published an editorial on December 31, 2015 on what trends to expect in 2016, it addressed a number of topics including: economic issues, technological advances, advances in science, fashion trends, social media trends and the political outlook.

Scarcely missed by those but a devoted few was any mention of trends developing in the charitable sector, the employer of more than two and a half million Canadians from one end of the country to another and worth more than the GDP of Pakistan.

It's hard to imagine that an industry spending $166 billion of public money and issuing $15.7 billion in official donation receipts can continue to run so far beneath the radar. But it does.

The whole state of affairs has taken on the appearance of a *Guinness World Book of Record* size case of "don't ask, don't tell."

And when it comes to the dynamics, the health and the effectiveness of the charitable sector, people outside the sector, as well as those who work inside it, seem at a loss as to what questions need to be asked and answered.

Pablo Eisenberg is a regular contributor to *The Chronicle of Philanthropy*, a U.S.-based magazine, which prints a monthly edition that has a circulation of around 25,000 that also operates a website. Eisenberg is an American scholar and social justice advocate who came from Paris to live in New Jersey with his parents at the age of seven, two years before the U.S. entered World War II. He is currently a senior Fellow at Georgetown University's Public Policy Institute. For 23 years, he was the executive director of the Center for Community Change, a Washington, D.C. organization that is "inspired by the conviction that we can create a society in which everyone has enough to thrive and achieve their full potential."

In a recent column, Mr. Eisenberg referred to the Oscar-winning movie *Spotlight*, which recounted the activities of the *Boston Globe's*, "Spotlight" investigative team and which wrote extensively about the abuse of children by Catholic priests. The same team did reporting on tax-exempt organizations in 2003 and 2004 that resulted in legislative changes.

But after more than four decades of working in the sector, Eisenberg says, "it's frustrating to realize how little investigative work is now done by the nation's mainstream newspapers, or by the growing number of nonprofit news organizations."

Instead, he says the media has largely been holding a love-in with philanthropy, especially its big donors.

"It is a shame that investigative-journalism outlets rarely consider nonprofits a worthy target of their investigations," he says. "An independent and healthy press has been one of the foundations of our democracy. No one should forget this."

3/

Our Cancer Future

If Alan Rickman, David Bowie and King Hussein of Jordan can die of cancer, then who in the world is safe?

Cancer is the leading cause of death worldwide. Eight million people died of cancer in 2012. It is a disease that drives us to perform arithmetical gymnastics like bookies at a racetrack, all in the hope of beating the odds.

Leaving the scientists to their work for a moment, the statistics available to drill down on cancer variables (real or imagined) would make the most sabermetrically-minded baseball fan's head spin.

Baseball statistics are cereal-box reading compared to the level of statistical variables related to cancer. For one thing, scientists tell us that cancer is an umbrella for more than 200 different diseases. Imagine having the body of existing baseball statistics multiplied for 200 other sports just like it. That will give you an idea of the numbers available for you to calculate your odds of getting or beating cancer.

Similarly, there are plenty of opportunities to debate the existence of the "meaningless cancer statistic," just like baseball fans argue about the meaningless baseball statistic. Does the "pitcher vs. batter match-up" stat really mean anything or is the sample size just too small? What about the RBI (runs batted in)? Or the increasingly used pitcher's WHIP (walks plus hits per inning pitched)? Will knowing this information hand you the lead in the baseball pool?

But, somewhat unlike statistically-driven baseball fans, there are a few things world cancer scientists actually do agree on. And here are some facts from the World Health Organization's (WHO) *World Cancer Report, 2014* that might be worth considering.

- Tobacco use is the single leading risk factor for cancer and is responsible for around 20 per cent of all cancer deaths globally.
- More than a third of cancer deaths—and possibly a

half according to other studies—can be "prevented or modified" by avoiding key risk factors such as smoking, using alcohol, being overweight, eating an unhealthy diet, lack of physical activity, infection by HPV (human papilloma virus), HBV (hepatitis B), ionizing and non-ionizing radiation, urban air pollution and indoor smoke from household use of fuels.

And what does the WHO say can be done to increase your odds of *avoiding* cancer? We can,

- Vaccinate against HBV and HPV.
- Avoid individual risk factors as best we can.
- Control occupational hazards.
- Reduce exposure to non-ionizing radiation by sunlight (UV) and reduce exposure to ionizing radiation (e.g. radon in homes or medical diagnostic imaging).

If you have cancer, your odds of *surviving* it are based on early detection, a correct diagnosis and effective treatment. Patient survival and quality of life are both considered in treatment plans.

Calculating your odds also depends upon the type of cancer you have and like baseball, there are many thousands of spreadsheets to assist in this endeavor, but bear in mind before you go down that path, there is the real risk of it driving you straight around the bend.

But while the availability of cancer statistics invites the metaphor of sabermetrics, at least to this author, the metaphor screeches to a halt when we start a conversation about money and cancer. Because there is far more known about the business of baseball than there is about the business of cancer.

The economy of cancer is more like a nebula—vast, indistinct and mostly incomprehensible—with only the occasional silhouette visible. And the ways in which cancer resources are assigned remain enigmatic.

It's tough to fill a black hole of information.

But some people are trying. In 2009, the Livestrong Foundation, a keen investor in cancer surveillance and cancer prevention initiatives, funded The Economist Intelligence Unit, an independent business unit within *The Economist* magazine that offers "bespoke modeling and scenario analysis" to look at the costs of cancer around the globe. They collaborated with academics and international cancer experts to publish a report, *Breakaway: The Global Burden of Cancer.*

The Intelligence Unit authors noted two firsts for the publication. One, being the first time "to their knowledge" that "the global economic burden of cancer has been converted to economic terms" and, two, it was the first time the cancer spending gap between developed and developing countries was quantified.

The report estimated that the costs associated with "new cancer cases diagnosed globally in 2009" was USD $286 billion and that number did not include the USD $19 billion it estimated was spent on cancer research in that year.

In 2014, the World Health Organization's (WHO's) *World Cancer Report* estimated the "total annual economic cost of cancer" at USD $1.16 trillion, more than 2 per cent of the global GDP. At the same time, the report said, "based on an initial review of the literature, there has never been a comprehensive body of work on the economics of the global cancer burden."

The Economist Intelligence Unit Report made one fact crystal clear.

Your best chance of beating the cancer odds is to be born in a developed country, where 95 per cent of global cancer resources are spent.

Only 5 per cent of global cancer resources are spent in developing countries. In this contrast, cancer is riding like an unstoppable wave across poorer parts of the world where more than half of the world's new cancer cases and three quarters of the world's cancer deaths occurred in 2009.

Lung cancer is the leading cause of cancer in the developed and the developing world. The adoption of Western lifestyles such as smoking is said to be responsible for the rise of lung cancer in poorer countries.

Cancers related to the growth of chronic infection are a mainstay of new cancer diagnosis in the developing world. Chronic infections such as hepatitis B and C are related to liver cancer. The H. Pylori virus is related to stomach cancer and the human papilloma virus (HPV) is related to cervical cancer. Kaposi sarcoma, a cancer associated with HIV/AIDS, is the second most common form of cancer for African men and the third most common cancer for African women.

The report estimated that 89 per cent of the world's cases of cervical cancer in 2009 would be diagnosed in the developing world, a cancer that is widely preventable in the developed world by the HPV vaccine.

The unbalanced distribution of the world's resources is not a new story. It's evidenced in the lack of education, opportunities lost and, of course, access to health care. And while the imbalance is shocking, there is the sense of why would we expect it to be any different. Despite million and billions and trillions of donations being thrown up against the wall of making the world a healthier place, inequity continues to persist. Why should the cancer economy be any different?

The assumption that charities are the appropriate delivers of health and social services and embody the essence of good works has enabled the charity sector to grow into a gargantuan spender of public funding and the second largest economic sector both in Canada and the U.S. with comparatively little transparency regarding coordinated action, priority setting and impact. That's not to say there isn't a lot of good work happening in cancer research charities, but it's tough to tell if it's the *best* kinds of work that can be done with the vast resources being invested.

So much of our response to the fear of contracting and surviving a frightening disease like cancer is to throw money at it in the hope that one more dollar will unlock the cure. We can thus, regardless of how the money is spent, believe that we are improving our odds. We believe this because we assume that the decisions being made and priorities being set in the cancer universe are the best decisions that can be made for the largest number of people.

But with the scarcity of quality information on the economy of cancer, (much of which exists within the transparency-starved economy of the charitable sector) the validity of that assumption might well be challenged, not just in Canada, but also in developed countries all over the world.

——

Dr. Christine Williams, Chief Mission Officer and Scientific Director of the Canadian Cancer Society (CCS) is as close as you could come to ground zero of cancer research in Canada.

She graduated from the University of Toronto with her PhD in Immunology in 1999. Her thesis, *DNA Damage Checkpoints in the Development of Normal and Neoplastic Lymphocytes*, explores the role of DNA repair pathways in the development of leukemia and lymphoma in children.

Wanting to keep her eyes on the purpose of her research, for the six years she was completing her PhD, she spent two weeks every summer as a counselor at a summer camp for children with cancer.

When she finished her dissertation, she moved to Boston with her husband and became a research fellow at Harvard University, continuing her work on DNA pathways and pediatric leukemia and lymphoma alongside immunologist, Katia Georgopoulos.

After five years of post-doctoral studies in a laboratory, she found herself at a crossroads. She felt she needed to make a choice. What would be the one direction she would pursue?

"Did I want to become a professor, pursue medical school or choose something outside academia? I needed to make a decision," she said.

External events tipped the balance. When her husband was offered a job in Toronto, she hung up her lab coat and took a position at the national peer-reviewed research program of Canadian Cancer Society Research Institute (formerly National Cancer Institute of Canada). Then, in 2009, she joined the Canadian Cancer Society as Vice-President of Research and became the Chief Mission Officer and Scientific Director in 2015.

And so it was that Dr. Christine Williams become the rare person working in a Canadian charity that had an overview of the entire cancer environment.

"In a landscape that is divided according to tumour sites, I get to look at the big picture," she says, "beyond a particular cancer or my specific organization."

"I'm looking at cancer research as a whole, including globally, to understand the initiatives and research trends, the emerging science, and where research and policy intersect. On top of that the Canadian

Cancer Society is delivering programs directly to people with cancer and their families. And that is an exceedingly rare mandate for a single organization," she says.

It's a safe bet that Christine would be the smartest person in the room on any given day. Her well-aimed, rapid-fire sentences, overflowing with facts, are delivered with surgical precision and, occasionally, irony. Cancer research can seem laden with irony. She seems relaxed in her role. Her smile is quick and wide.

She has just finished up three years as co-chair of the Canadian Cancer Research Alliance (CCRA).

A coordinated approach to cancer research is only beginning to emerge in Canada. The CCRA evolved from one of the early advisory groups to the Canadian Strategy for Cancer Control and its Executive Office is supported by the Canadian Partnership Against Cancer, a federally funded not for profit, charged with leading Canada's cancer control strategy. The activities of the CCRA are directed by a board, consisting of representatives from the major cancer research funders in Canada.

The CCRA has 35 members. They are government funding agencies, provincial care providers and charities involved in cancer research funding and they range from the largest government funder of cancer research, the Canadian Institute of Health Research, that contributed $141 million in 2013, to Ovarian Cancer Canada, which contributed $191 thousand that same year.

The Canadian Cancer Research Alliance is the one body in Canada that is tracking where cancer research money is spent, defining cancer research priorities and creating the partnerships to fund those priorities.

According to Kim Badovinac, the Manager of Canadian Cancer Research Survey with the Canadian Cancer Research Alliance, the

CCRA initiated its survey because they had hunches that certain areas of research (like prevention) and certain cancers (like lung cancer) weren't being well-funded. But no one really knew precisely where the funding was going. The 23 foundational members of the CCRA pooled their resources to hire Kim to start gathering data about the kinds of cancer research being funded.

Members began to pool their research funding data. The first report, *The Canadian Cancer Research Alliance's Survey Of Government And Voluntary Sector Investment In Cancer Research in 2005,* was published in 2007.

Dr. Philip Branton was the Scientific Director of the Institute of Cancer Research at the Canadian Institutes of Health Research and the Gilman Cheney Professor of Biochemistry at McGill University at the time. He was CCRA's inaugural chairperson and a driving force behind the initiation of the survey. He said the report, "helped to elucidate what we anecdotally suspected, namely, that studies of some types of cancers likely require more funding, that more investment in studies designed to understand the causes of cancer and how to prevent cancer are needed, and that the conduct of cancer research is fairly concentrated in key centres in the country."

Kim has been involved in researching and writing that report and in every report the CCRA has issued since with advisors like Christine helping in the effort. The scope of the survey has been expanded beyond CCRA members and now includes 42 organizations involved in cancer research funding.

"In the past ten years, there has been an effort to coordinate cancer research activities," says Christine. "I've worked in a health charities coalition and with other non-cancer groups and now there's a certain amount of cancer organization "envy" because the sector is becoming more coordinated and there's willingness to share data and information between the research funding organizations, in particular. Canada now has a foundation of a collaborative strategic cancer research-funding plan."

In 2013, the survey reported that $498 million was awarded.

Figure 3.1 shows the contribution of funds from federal, provincial and charitable partners. Figure 3.2 shows the contribution of the charitable members of the CCRA. Figure 3.3 shows the trend of investment between 2005 and 2013 from federal, provincial and charitable partners. All the information is based on data from the CCRA.

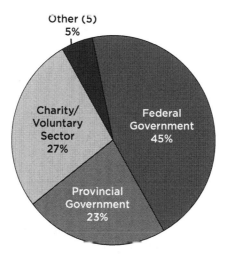

Figure 3.1: Cancer research investment by participating organizations/programs, 2013 ($498.2 million).

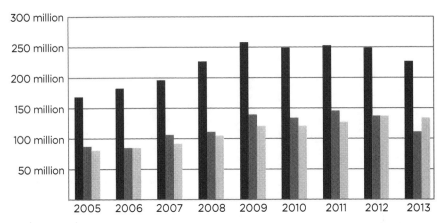

Figure 3.2: Trend of cancer research investment by participating organizations, 2005-2013.

Although the $498 million of research funding invested by CCRA members in 2013 provides a reasonable understanding of Canadian cancer research funding priorities, the entirety of cancer research funding in Canada involves players that are not members of the CCRA.

Pharmaceutical companies do not participate in the alliance so none of the research money they spend is included in the CCRA's 2013 $498 million figure. Their specific cancer research funding priorities are not public and naturally involve the development of new drugs.

Hospital foundations are not members of the alliance. The Princess Margaret Cancer Foundation and Sick Kids Foundation, for example, are not participating, yet they are big players on the cancer research scene.

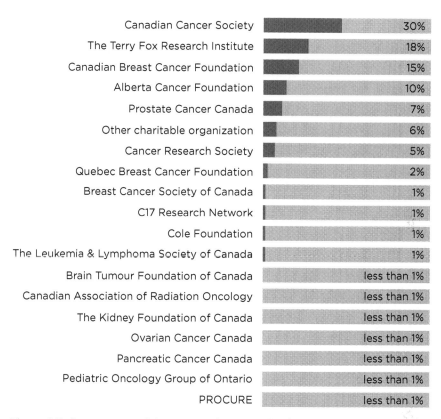

Figure 3.3: Cancer research investment by charitable/voluntary sector member organizations ($133.1 million).

"We've talked to them many times and had lots of meetings," says Christine Williams. "The issue is that the requirement of entry into the CCRA is data sharing. You have to share the data on where you are spending your research funds, on what projects, and what you are doing in terms of peered-reviewed research funding."

"We kind of go back and forth on whether they are either reluctant to share their data or they simply don't have it. I think it's probably more the latter—it requires a lot of tracking."

"It's the same thing with Sick Kids," offers Kim Badovinac.

"We know about 25 per cent of Sick Kids' research is on childhood cancer, but similar to Princess Margaret, we've never been able to get them to the table with research granting data. It may be that the data they have on their research grants is not in a readily packaged format for use in our survey."

"But even though these organizations are not members of CCRA," emphasizes Christine, "they are still an important part of the research environment."

An observer might wonder how it could possibly be that charities which raise hundreds of millions of dollars on behalf of cancer research, and issue hundreds of millions of dollars in federal tax credits, can *not* participate in a national initiative to coordinate the spending of billions of dollars of the people's money on cancer research. What reasons could there be for not being able to share data on the nature of the research projects those funds are supporting?

Ted Garrard, CEO of the Hospital for Sick Children Foundation, which raised CAD $172.4 million in 2013 says he "wouldn't have any comment on that because participation in that Alliance would be driven through the Sick Kids Institute, not through the Foundation."

But, he says, that "any research grant that somebody at our research institute seeks is internally peer-reviewed first; any amount over $50,000 is internally peer-reviewed. All of the grants we get are externally peer-reviewed."

The Sick Kids Research Institute (the Peter Gilgan Centre for Research and Learning) is currently running 1,200 different research programs decided upon by the Institute under the jurisdiction of the Sick Kids' Board of Directors and had expenditures of $181.5 million in 2015.

Paul Alofs, CEO of the Princess Margaret Cancer Foundation,

which raised CAD $177.3 million in 2013, and is currently in the last year of its $1 billion personalized medicine campaign *Believe It!* declined to be interviewed for this book.

—•—

Oncology is the main driver in precision medicine. It's happening in other diseases, but cancer drugs and treatment is driving the focus on precision treatment, and that means the treatment will be more expensive per patient. According to Christine Williams, the last thing the cancer care agencies and health services providers may want to hear about is precision medicine. More standardized treatments are easier to deliver and less expensive. This introduces a potential conflict between the direction research is taking us and what health care systems can afford to pay.

"Ironically, for charities like the Canadian Cancer Society, our biggest fundraising competitors are not other charities so much as they are big hospital foundations."

"It's funny because on the fundraising side, it's competitive, but on the research funding side, it's collaborative and you see partnerships all over the place."

While the Canadian Cancer Research Alliance is the major cancer player on the Canadian national cancer research scene, the Canadian Partnership Against Cancer, (the Partnership) is "an independent organization funded by the federal government to accelerate action on cancer control for all Canadians." It works with cancer experts, charitable organizations, governments, cancer agencies, national health organizations, patients, survivors and others to implement Canada's cancer control strategy.

The *Canada Health Act* makes provinces the boss on matters of delivering health care so special coordinating initiatives are necessary to find out what's happening on a provincial level and then, ideally, develop a national strategy.

The Partnership's mandate focuses on collaboration with as many cancer organizations as possible throughout the country. The work of the CCRA, which preceded the formation of the Partnership, now falls under the Partnership umbrella.

There are three basic statistics when it comes to cancer in Canada and they are based on cancer modeling programs developed by the Public Health Agency of Canada (PHAC) and used by the Canadian Cancer Society.

1. *40 per cent of Canadians will get cancer at some time in their life span.* That means if you live to an average Canadian life span of 82 years, there is a 40 per cent chance of contracting the disease. Your odds increase the older you get. Not a pleasant thought unless you consider the alternative. But age really does make the difference.

   ◦ 89% of cancers are diagnosed in people over the age of 50;
   ◦ 18% will occur in people aged 50-59;
   ◦ 28% in people aged 60-69, and
   ◦ 43% in people over the age of 70.

2. *The overall 5-year cancer survival rate has increased in Canada to 63 per cent compared to the survival of comparable people in the general population, but that ranges widely by the type of cancer.* Survival is not a cure. It is survival. And 63 per cent is an average across all cancer types.

3. *The increasingly aged population and the increased number of people who are surviving cancer due to modern treatment means that the number of people in Canada walking around with cancer will increase by 71 per cent to 2.2 million people in the next 15 years.* The impact of that number is mind bending if you take into consideration the fact that one hospital in North Toronto sees 1,300 patients for chemotherapy treatment every day. With a 71 per cent increase, they could be seeing 2,223 people a day.

How will that kind of growth be managed? And paid for?

Perhaps in fifteen years, an ambitious researcher will have received funding for portable chemotherapy gear so people can walk around like they do with their oxygen tanks now. And, like the setting of a twisted futuristic cable series, people in treatment for cancer can sportingly sit at a Starbucks, their heads gaily turbaned, sipping a latte and pecking away at their mobile devices while chemotherapy drugs charge into their systems.

Whatever way you look at it, having 2.2 million people walking around with cancer is an expensive proposition, but there doesn't seem to be much research activity in trying to figure that out.

"I'm sure it's keeping a lot of people awake at night," says Christine Williams. "It's not that I don't think it's being worked on, but we've had trouble getting this data."

Cindy Gauvreau is employed at the Canadian Partnership Against Cancer as a Specialist in Health Economics.

She was raised in Vernon, B.C., received her undergraduate degree from the University of Victoria, did her masters in economics at the University of Toronto and received her PhD from U of T.

"I trained in health services research, but my own personal focus is on prevention. I have a background in infectious disease, which led me down the path of preventable disease and programs that are in the prevention area," she says.

Health economics is a relatively new field of economics and Cindy says that health economists look at (among other things) socio-economic drivers for people who seek medical help in the first place. Why, for example, would someone choose to go to an emergency room as opposed to going to a family doctor as opposed to going to a walk-in clinic?

There are also health economists who study the impact of health financing and how our insurance plans work. And then, in Canada's case, health economists work at the provincial level to help policy makers decide what programs make sense for their province and how they align with provincial policy objectives and fit in with the budget they have.

"From the health economist's point of view, you want to know how today's investment dollar will positively impact health outcomes in the future," Cindy clarifies.

"And you also want, in the gold standard of decision-making, for the decision to be made that impacts as many people as possible. So if the question is whether you are going to fund a drug that's fantastically expensive and lifesaving but only gives you five lives, as opposed to paying for a vaccine program for HPV, for cervical cancer that is going to affect a far larger number of people, how will you choose. That's the balance that has to be met."

But Cindy says that looking for *the* number (the big number for Canada about the costs of cancer 15 years from now) might be good for public relations, but that it would be missing the point.

"The big number is shocking and raises awareness for the public, but in the end, there needs to be some kind of tool to prioritize spending," she says.

There are other pressures on governments. You can't fund every prevention initiative, even though that is what will save costs down the road.

"Some cancers are very slow moving," she says. "Lung cancer takes 15 years to develop. And maybe the decision-maker has to make a decision this year on whether it will fund mental health services. So those are the kinds of things health economists help to decide on. It's not just simply the cost. It's the priorities."

That's one more reason, one could argue, to make sure that we have the information we need to make sure the resources we are currently spending (a vast majority of them by charities) are being allocated in a way that helps the most people, now and in the future.

———

"There's a lot of things we are doing in health care that we could probably stop doing," says Christine Williams. She is talking about the increasing interest in de-implementation science.

"It particularly comes up in drug access," she says. "We pride ourselves on being evidence-based organizations. You've heard the federal government making lots of noise about being evidence-based policy makers. Given that we believe in evidence, there should also be evidence about what doesn't work. We've been starting to talk with some other agencies about some sort of funding opportunity in de-implementation so that waste can be taken out of the system. How do we get the evidence to show that? How do we get the stuff that's not working off the formulary and off the clinical protocols?"

The Partnership reports, as well as the Canadian Cancer Society reports, and reports from the Public Health Agency of Canada underline the importance of prioritizing prevention. According to its 2012-17 strategic plan, the Partnership lists the development of "high-impact, population-based prevention and cancer screening approaches" at the top of its priorities and says that if half of the 21 per cent of Canadians who smoke quit, an estimated 45,000 people would be prevented from developing lung cancer, an estimated 33,000 deaths from lung cancer would be avoided, as would $947 million in treatment costs.

The WHO's *World Cancer Report 2014* also states, "cancer can be reduced and controlled by implementing evidence-based strategies for cancer prevention."

But in order to get to the place where we can fully factor prevention research into the odds of beating cancer in Canada, we need to take a wide view of that cancer research nebula to see the silhouette of how cancer research is being prioritized.

Figure 3.4 is based on data from the Canadian Cancer Research Alliance. The three bars each represent a cancer site (bladder, bone, brain or breast, for example) and are grouped together to represent incidence, mortality and prevalence of a site-specific cancer.

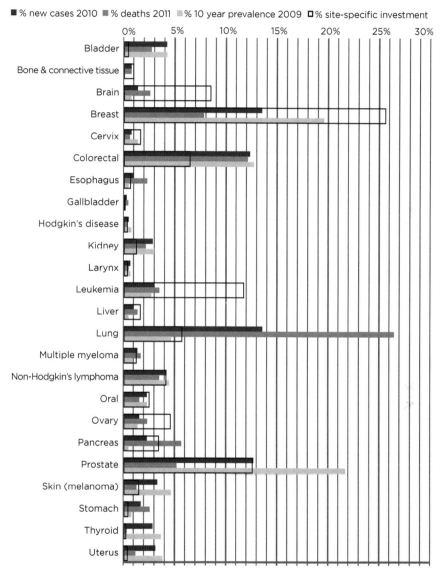

Figure 3.4: Distribution of 2013 site-specific cancer research investment ($288.7 m) by new cancer cases in 2010, cancer deaths in 2011 and 10-year prevalence in selected cancer sites.

The first horizontal bar, (dark grey) reflects the *incidence* of that particular kind of cancer as a percentage of the all the cancers diagnosed in 2010. For example, you can see that fewer than 5 per cent of cancers diagnosed in 2010 were bladder cancer and that almost 14 per cent of cancers diagnosed in 2010 were lung cancer.

The second bar, (medium grey) represents the percentage of deaths from that particular kind of cancer as a percentage of deaths of all kinds of cancer in 2011. The deaths are not necessarily the same people diagnosed in 2010, but represent the number of people who died from that type of cancer in 2011. They could have been diagnosed in 2010 or any year prior to that, but they passed away in 2011. You can see that more than 25 per cent of all cancer deaths in 2011 were from lung cancer, about 12 per cent of cancer deaths in 2011 were from colorectal cancer, less than 7 per cent of cancer deaths in 2011 were from breast cancer and 5 per cent from prostate cancer.

The third bar (light grey) lets you know about the *prevalence* of a particular type of cancer. The Cancer Quality Control Council of Ontario defines prevalence as "both the number of people in a population who have been diagnosed with cancer in a given time period and those who are still alive on a given date. It includes both new (incident) and existing cases, and it is determined by both incidence and survival."

It essentially means that if you were to run into someone who had cancer ten years ago, they would most likely be a breast or prostate cancer survivor. (On the graph you'll see prevalence of breast cancer at just under 20 per cent and prevalence of prostate cancer at just over 20 per cent.) Despite the fact that lung cancer is the most common cancer diagnosis, fewer than 5 per cent of people surviving cancer ten years more have lung cancer.

High mortality relates to low prevalence.

The fourth piece of information overlaid on this chart represented by the black outline, is the percentage of research investment in the specific types of cancer identified on the chart. The total amount of site-specific research conducted by CCRA members in 2013 was CAD $288.7 million.

You will likely note, that the percentage of research is *not* correlated to incidence, mortality or prevalence.

Lung cancer, the most common cancer in Canada with the highest mortality rate receives about 6 per cent of site-specific cancer funding. Breast cancer, on the other hand, while the incidence is at about 14 per cent of all cancers, with a mortality rate of about 7 per cent of all cancers, receives more than 25 per cent of site-specific research investment. Brain cancer and leukemia also fall into this category. While brain cancer accounts for less than 2 per cent of all cancer, it receives about 8 per cent of the site-specific research investment. Leukemia with about a 3 per cent incidence receives about 12 per cent of the site-specific research investment. Non site-specific research encompasses projects that are relevant to more than one type of cancer.

There are several explanations offered for this dynamic. One is that people who get cancer and live to tell the tale are more able to support fundraising efforts for research. Other people say that cancers affecting younger people—brain, breast, leukemia and prostate—are more "sellable."

Charities are often leading the charge on the marketing piece of cancer research. And, basically, whoever is doing the best marketing job is making the money. And because of the way charities operate, you only need to take care of who is under your umbrella. The weather beyond that is someone else's responsibility.

"The other way to look at this is that every cancer should be funded like breast cancer," says Christine Williams, "and that this is actually how we make a change in the five-year survival rate in cancers like pancreatic cancer that need more attention, more research funding. There's no doubt if you put more money into it, you will make change in the five-year survival rate."

But survival rates are another sticky thing when it comes to cancer statistics and our ongoing calculation of beating the odds.

One of the big questions is, what does *surviving* cancer exactly mean?

Elaine Wong is a young woman who works in the charitable sector and is currently doing her Masters in Public Policy at Dalhousie University. She is also, to her great credit, helping with the research on this book. She talks about her father's experience.

My dad was diagnosed with nasopharyngeal cancer when he was 43. We'd never heard of this type of cancer before and it was fairly aggressive. He went through the usual chemo and radiation at Princess Margaret and Sunnybrook hospitals, but the cancer came back. He and my mom sought out specialists in Hong Kong with more experience and they went back and forth to Hong Kong a few times for treatment but nothing worked. All this took place over five years from diagnosis to his passing. The last two years were especially tough because he just slowly wasted away. Physical deterioration is one thing, but my dad really loved to read, learn, and discuss and debate with his friends and family about…everything! When he couldn't do that anymore or think as clearly or quickly the way he did, it really took a piece of his identity away. He was just a shell of the man I knew and admired growing up, and that was hard on him and on us as a family.

Technically he survived and would be counted in the five-year survival statistics, but I know towards the end, he wondered if the treatments were worth it because it felt as though the treatments did a lot worse than the actual cancer.

"This is true what your researcher went through...absolutely," says Christine. "And in pediatric cancer we treat cancers like medulloblastoma, little kids with brain tumours, by radiating their brains. And then, in the worse case scenarios, they can become almost in a vegetative state, hunched over and might never grow to full stature and their intellect is massively impacted, but they're survivors and they count in the survival rate."

"So, absolutely, we are aware and sensitive to some of those issues. And then you have other people like breast cancer survivors who are like unbelievable dynamic members of society and just getting on with their lives. But that's why our whole research program includes quality of life research."

Another thing these graphs don't show is that—despite the coordinated efforts of the Canadian Cancer Research Alliance, and the unequivocally stated prevention priorities of the World Health Organization, Canadian Partnership Against Cancer and many

more international cancer authorities all identifying cancer prevention initiatives—less than 10 per cent of the $498 million CCRA
members invested in cancer research in 2013 was devoted to cancer
prevention.

Christine Williams says the biggest problem is capacity.

"We've learned this the hard way," she says. "We tried to fund
more research through open grant programs in prevention, but then
actually realized there weren't the researchers to do it. The strength
in Canada is in the bio-medical, translational science community.
Prevention just hasn't been a big area of emphasis. We need to build
the community."

People are still very afraid of a cancer diagnosis and fear is a very
powerful motivating force, so the emphasis on cancer is about curing
it. The National Cancer Act that President Nixon passed in 1971 was
about putting $1.6 billion into cancer research in the U.S. which, at
the time, was a lot of money, and that was research for a cure. Cancer
research is very cure-oriented and it wasn't recognized for a long
time what a high percentage of cancers is actually preventable.

Prevention research funding has been a strategic priority of the
Canadian Cancer Society for the last five years. But prevention is
hard to fundraise for and one of the challenges about prevention is
proving that it works.

"The Canadian Cancer Society's own brand studies show there
is huge brand recognition, and everybody knows what the yellow
daffodils are all about," says Christine. "Our message is organic like
'we're trying to stop cancer before it starts' or 'we're trying to end
cancer.'"

"But the Canadian Cancer Society raises money $20 at a time,"
says Christine. "Small donations are the bulk of our fundraising. Increasingly, like everyone else, we are trying to target major

donors, and that's a different conversation. You are really talking to them about what *their* interests are and how they intersect with the Society's mission. Some donors are interested in prevention and some donors are not, so the conversations are tailored to that."

4 /

Let's *Not* Take That Cancer Journey

In Canada close to nine million people, almost a third of the population, depend on untreated ground water for drinking.

"In Nova Scotia, 45 per cent of households rely on well water," said Dr. Louise Parker in 2014 on the day she launched a Nova Scotia study on the possible connection between arsenic from water wells and the higher than average cancer rates experienced by that province.

Dr. Parker is a world-renowned epidemiologist. She came to Nova Scotia from the University of Newcastle in the United Kingdom where she was founding Director of the Paediatric and Lifecourse Epidemiology Faculty Research Group, the Head of Child Health, and Deputy Head of the School of Clinical Medical Sciences. She was also the Associate Director of Research and Development at the National Institute for Clinical Excellence in London at the time.

She had published more than 165 peer-reviewed research papers, served on the editorial boards of several major journals, and was editor in chief of *Pediatric Hematology Oncology* from 2000 to 2006.

The abstract for one of her studies, *Understanding the translation of scientific knowledge about arsenic risk exposure among private well water users in Nova Scotia*, states that "Arsenic is a class I human carcinogen that has been identified as the second most important global health concern in groundwater supplies after contamination by pathogenic organisms. Hydrogeological assessments have shown naturally occurring arsenic to be widespread in groundwater across the northeastern United States and eastern Canada. Knowledge of arsenic risk exposure among private well users in these arsenic endemic areas has not yet been fully explored but research on water quality perceptions indicates a consistent misalignment between public and scientific assessments of environmental risk."

"Arsenic is a known carcinogen and increases the rates of several cancers, including that of the bladder and kidney," says Dr. Parker in a voice with an equal measure of a comforting British accent and the steely intention of a woman who wants to be fully understood. "Arsenic is a natural contaminant of many water supply wells in Nova Scotia, and we wanted to find out whether drinking arsenic-contaminated water is one of the reasons the rates of bladder and kidney cancer are higher in Atlantic Canada than most of the rest of Canada."

Louise Parker was considered a great "catch" in the research world when she came to work in Canada. She was lured across the pond with the offer of the Canadian Cancer Society (Nova Scotia Division) Chair in Population Cancer Research at Dalhousie University and the opportunity to head up the $7 million Atlantic Partnership for Tomorrow's Health (PATH) study, a long-term population health study of the genetic, lifestyle and environmental factors behind the region's high cancer rates.

Dr. Parker upped the ante for the PATH study. In addition to the information gleaned from the questionnaires, the venous blood samples and the DNA samples collected from the cohort, she added toenails to the list of what she wanted collected from Atlantic Canadians. The nail samples would reveal the amount of arsenic being ingested by people living in that area.

The PATH study is Atlantic Canada's contribution to the gathering of data on a cohort of 300,000 Canadians that, through questionnaires, gathers lifestyle, diet, physical activity, medications and other information. About 145,000 blood samples have been gathered and follow-up surveys will be conducted over time.

The overall cohort, called Canadian Partnership for Tomorrow (CPTP), is the single largest piece of infrastructure built around the identification of cancer risk factors in Canada. CPTP is the Canadian Partnership Against Cancer's single largest investment.

Luca Pisterzi is a Program Manager in the National Coordination Centre for the CPTP. His previous work was with the Ontario Brain Institute and he tells me his PhD is not in cancer. It's actually in signaling proteins, which turn things on and off, he says, so those proteins are ubiquitous. They are all over the body. Some of them are implicated in cancer.

"I was a scientist who saw CPTP as really exciting," says Luca. "I see the value of getting exposed to these big data approaches to science. It can be used very effectively and it has a lot of potential for researchers and patients."

"The idea with CPTP is, once there are enough data points, you can go back and look at the risk factors that could have contributed to people developing cancer. It lends itself to the research of cancer and chronic diseases."

CPTP joins other global longitudinal health studies like the Nurses' Study in the United States, which has been following more than 120,000 female nurses since 1976 to assess risk factors for cancer and cardiovascular disease, and the European Prospective Investigation into Cancer and Nutrition (EPIC) study, which has been active since 2000. It is spread across ten countries in Europe, involves more than 500,000 people and focuses on nutrition and cancer.

According to Luca, the other cohort studies around the world are doing different things, and that Canada needs its own cohort for a number of reasons.

"We have a lot of unique exposures in Canada," he tells me. "Even if you look at a province like B.C., you've got a lot of diversity. There's north/south geographic diversity and environmental diversity. There is a gradient across Canada in terms of cancer incidence from east to west. We have a very ethnically diverse population and are very genetically diverse. We're a unique country in that way. So, while there might be a similar study, let's say, going on in Denmark, they are more homogeneous in terms of population, geography and environment. We have a lot of unique exposures."

CPTP is a partnership of five regional cohorts: the B.C. Generations Project in British Columbia, Alberta's Tomorrow Project in Alberta, the Ontario Health Study in Ontario, CartaGen in Quebec and Atlantic PATH (Partnership for Tomorrow's Health) in the four Atlantic provinces.

Dr. Parker and her team raised the funding—a three-year grant of $575,000 from the Canadian Cancer Society—for the study and collected the nail clippings. They ended up getting 27,000 samples—and a mention in the *Guinness World Book of Records*.

"My team had looked at the Guinness website and while there were other toenail records—for example, the longest toenails—there wasn't a record for the largest collection of clippings. We thought it was a great opportunity to have a bit of fun after everyone's hard work and commitment to the project."

The team had the resources to measure the arsenic levels of 3,000 of the samples they collected.

One of the findings from the study was that body fat plays a role in how arsenic is absorbed into the body. In particular, women with higher levels of fat are less likely to retain arsenic in their body.

"We'd like to measure the presence of other elements such as lead, mercury and selenium and are seeking funding to do that and to work on mitigating the arsenic exposure. But we have tried and tried and tried to get funding for this work," she said. "And we have failed."

Echoing Dr. Christine Williams' observation of the cancer prevention research area as lacking the researchers experienced to conduct the work, Dr. Parker said, "the peer reviewers have no idea about prevention research and we've had bizarre reviews from panels who don't understand at all what we are trying to do. People don't understand prevention research...and the idea hasn't been sold."

Dr. Parker makes the point that research by tumor site, which is how most cancer research is organized, has very little to do with prevention. She believes is has more to do with the people who survive their diagnosis and treatment, the ones who are alive to tell their stories, providing the human interest angle needed to market and fundraise for the research.

"We can study the people who survive and they talk about their disease," she says. "Overall funding of medical research in general and, in particular, with cancer is looking for a cure. This is particularly well-established in North American and Europe," she says.

She also suggests that there's more money to be made from research for a cure than research prevention. "Research for a cancer cure involves patenting new products, new pharmaceuticals and the opportunity to play with 'sexy new studies.'"

The Canadian Cancer Research Alliance issued a report in 2013, *Investment in Cancer Risk & Prevention, 2005-2010* that shows how prevention initiatives are funded within the context of cancer research.

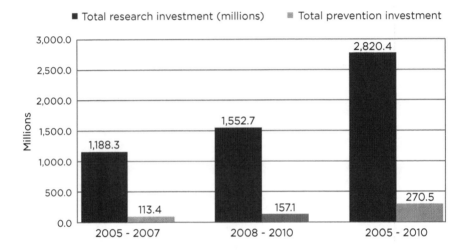

Figure 4.1: Prevention research as a portion of overall research, 2005–2010. 9.87% as reported in the CCRA Survey.

Of the $2.82 billion dollars spent on cancer research in Canada between 2005 and 2010, $270.5 million was spent on prevention initiatives. Tumour site drives 72 per cent of research funding in the area of prevention.

A government agency research funder, the Canadian Institute for Health Research (CIHR), was the main funder for prevention research, contributing 49 per cent between 2005 and 2010. The Canadian Cancer Society was the biggest charitable funder.

Within that $270.5 million bucket of prevention research funding, the amount devoted to researching contaminants in the air, water and soil—the kind of research Dr. Louise Parker is under-taking—is $17.5 million or 6.47 per cent. And that funding has remained flat-lined.

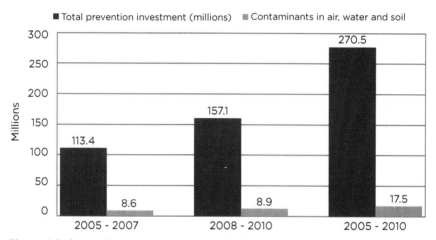

■ Total prevention investment (millions) ■ Contaminants in air, water and soil

Figure 4.2: Contaminants in air, water and soil as a portion of prevention research in Canada. 6.47% as reported in the CCRA Survey.

Dr. Parker believes the marketing of cancer research has a great deal of influence on the way research is resourced.

"There is little will in the nonprofit sector to get away from lab science. The pharmaceutical companies and medical suppliers have done a great job in convincing people that is where the progress lies. But for reasons of comfort and prejudice, lab science is more readily seen as fundable. It's very disappointing."

"The core of the issue of marketing cancer as caused by lifestyle is saying, 'it's your fault.' It's easier to say 'fight back'. But we need to start 'fighting back before it starts'," she emphasizes. "Because indi-viduals don't necessarily have the tools or the controls over what they are exposed to and something has to be done about that."

Dr. Parker's frustration with the lack of focus and funding on cancer prevention—and on her own teams' battle to get their arsenic research funded—makes her work grueling, she says.

"The main challenge is the lack of understanding," she says. "And the need to join strengths among researchers, health promotion people and legislators. Everyone is working in silos. Cancer prevention is like other disease prevention. It's swamped by short-termism, by narrow-minded and short-term thinking by people in decision-making positions, especially at the provincial level."

Dr. Parker, despite her distinguished career, is about to throw in the towel.

"When I filled the Chair in Populations Studies, I didn't realize how behind Canada was in its prevention research. It came as quite a shock and was a great disappointment to me. Canada needs a national strategy, but Canada doesn't do national strategies. There is a disparity of interests in the provinces."

"Prevention research doesn't involve fancy-dancy laboratories. Prevention involves people, not patients, and who wants to pay for them?"

"I have had enough. I'm retiring next year. The lack of expert review and the scarcity of funding— it's not worth the effort. I've had a successful career, but this has worn me down."

—·—

I am sitting at a café-sized table in the somewhat cramped office of Dr. Paul Demers. Similar to the other surfaces in his office, our little table is covered with stacks of files, papers and journals.

Paul is the Director of the Occupational Cancer Research Centre (OCRC) and was recruited to the OCRC from the University of British Columbia, where he was a Professor in the School of Environmental Health. He has an MSc in Industrial Hygiene and a PhD in Epidemiology, both from the University of Washington in Seattle.

Recognized as a global expert in occupational cancer risk, Paul has sat on several expert panels, including the International Agency for Research on Cancer (IARC) working groups that evaluate carcinogens. He is the Scientific Director at CAREX Canada, a "national surveillance project that estimates the number of Canadians exposed to substances associated with cancer in workplace and community environments."

In addition to being director of the OCRC, he is also currently a Professor at the University of Toronto's Dalla Lana School of Public Health.

"When I was offered the position as Director of the OCRC, I saw it as an opportunity to help create something of lasting importance," he says.

And even though occupational cancer research has been in decline since the Centre was established in 2009, he said he was drawn to the OCRC by the strong commitment of funders and stakeholders to reverse that trend, and take a leading role in this area of research. The Centre was established with funding from Cancer Care Ontario, the Canadian Cancer Society, and the Workplace Safety and Insurance Board (WSIB), and support from the United Steelworkers Union. The Ontario Ministry of Labour has since replaced the WSIB as a funder.

"Funding is a constant challenge. One of our charges for this centre is to build capacity in this area because it's been dwindling in recent years."

Paul puts the diminishing interest in occupational and

environmental exposures partly down to demographic shifts. He says there is a baby boomer generation that came of age during fall-out from Rachel Carson's 1962 book, *Silent Spring*, which reveals the impact of the indiscriminate use of pesticides and, in particular, DDT. The book became a rallying cry for the environmental movement that took hold in the 1960s.

"Occupational and environmental health research were hand-in-hand and there was a generation of researchers that came to the forefront in that period," he says. "I came in at the tail end of it. That generation is hitting retirement age now and we aren't the sexy new area to become involved with any longer. And without environmental and occupational hazards being priority areas for funding, attracting new people and building capacity is difficult."

The Occupational Cancer Research Centre states that around sixty occupational exposures have been classified as "definite or probable" human carcinogens. There are more than a hundred other and that many workplace substances that cause cancer in animals that have not been studied in humans.

"The front line of environmental protection is the workplace, where the levels of hazard are much, much higher," says Paul.

Occupational cancer researchers believe that occupational exposures could account for 20-30 per cent of the cancers among people who work in trades such as agriculture, construction, mining, welding and protective services.

Of the $270.5 million invested in cancer prevention research by Canadian Cancer Research Alliance members, $3.5 million or 1.29 per cent of that was invested into the study of occupational risk factors. There were 23 Principal Investigators (PIs) who were involved in projects focusing on Occupational Exposures over the six years of the study.

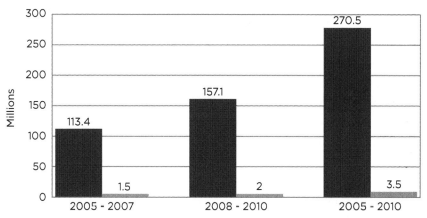

- Total prevention investment (millions) 2005 - 2010
- Investment in occupational exposures as factors

Figure 4.3: Occupational exposures as a portion of prevention research in Canada, 2005 - 2010. 1.29% as reported in the CCRA Survey.

"Part of it is we can't rely upon the standard granting agencies," says Paul Demers. "We have to think outside the box and really push for funding wherever we can. A lot of the funding that I receive is not where other people necessarily receive funding. I've gotten the International Development Research Centre to fund some of our work with the Pan-American Health Organization. The Canadian Nuclear Safety Commission funds our work on uranium miners."

In some quarters, there's an idea that cancer deaths from occupational exposure is low compared to other forms of cancers.

"I guess it depends on what you consider to be low," says Paul. "It's higher compared to car accidents and yet we consider car accidents to be important. And it's probably higher compared to HIV/AIDS right now. So, it depends on your criteria for high versus low. It's lower than smoking, indeed, but there's nothing higher than smoking for cancer risk."

Figures recently released by the Institute for Work & Health, which receives its core funding from the province of Ontario, shows the cost of asbestos-related cancers to be at the $1.7 billion mark. The average cost per person of cancers and mesothelioma related to workplace exposure to asbestos is $818,000.

The Ontario Occupational Cancer Research Centre sits in office space donated by Cancer Care Ontario (CCO), which also covers Paul's salary. He estimates the annual budget of his Centre, including the value of the rent and salary contribution by CCO, and other gifts-in-kind, to be between two and two and a half million dollars a year.

"We're one of the larger occupational centres in the country in that way," he says.

What would Paul do if he had a budget of $10 million, 2 per cent of the cancer research funds spent by CCRA members in 2013?

"I've never thought about it in terms of blue sky like that," he says, betraying a well-earned sense of futility in dreaming big.

"If I had $10 million I didn't have to beg and scrape for on an annual basis that would certainly give us an infrastructure to move forward. A challenge in Canada is that we don't have any targeted federal funding for occupational health research. We are under provincial jurisdiction. The federal government doesn't have an institute focused in on this, and it's true for the environment as well."

It's a short-term vision considering that many our causes of cancer actually cause other forms of chronic disease too.

But Paul has another problem that keeps nagging at him.

"Every day I walk by these signs. You probably know the ones. One says 'The answer is in your genes' and draped in front of that, there's one that's all about the 'patient's journey' or the 'cancer journey' and things like that. Our informal slogan is around here is 'let's stop that journey. Let's not go there at all.'"

The problem is that prevention is more of a long view because of the length of time it takes to develop cancer. But the fact is, the long view is the view that needs to get taken. That's not to say that some of these other efforts that people are supporting around better diet and exercise — those are also going to contribute in the long run — but there's less of a willingness to look at some of these preventable occupational risk factors because it might lead to controversy or other things.

"There are economic consequences," says Paul Demers. "Look at the recent glyphosate controversy internationally. Glyphosate is a herbicide and Roundup is the primary commercial product. It's one of the largest volume pesticides in the world and has just been classified as a probable human carcinogen by the International Agency for Research on Cancer (IARC). Monsanto owns Roundup and is very upset."

Monsanto called the IARC conclusion "inconsistent with decades of ongoing comprehensive safety assessments."

The U.S. Environmental Protection Agency had determined that the science "does not provide evidence to show that glyphosate causes cancer." But now the EPA says it will analyze new findings by the IARC.

"There are economic and political consequences of saying okay, we have to reduce exposure to carcinogens," says Paul.

—·—

If the studies of Contaminants in the Air, Water and Soil and Occupational Exposures are the poor cousins of risk factors in the cancer prevention research universe, which, remember, is already a poor cousin of cancer research in general, then the research around alcohol as a risk factor is the most destitute poverty-stricken cousin of all.

Alcohol was classified as a Group 1 carcinogen by the International Agency for Research into Cancer (IARC) in 1988. A study published by Cancer Research UK in 2011 found that alcohol is responsible for about 4 per cent of UK cancers or 12,800 cases per year. The study reports that "upper aero-digestive tract cancers (oral cavity and pharynx, larynx, and oesophageal) have the highest proportions of cases linked to alcohol consumption, but bowel cancers accounted for the greatest overall number of cases linked to alcohol (around 4,800 cases a year)."

Yet, in Canada, from 2005–2010, less than $1 million was invested in studying alcohol as a risk factor for cancer.

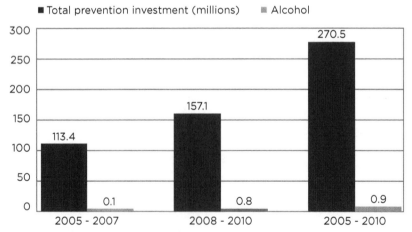

Figure 4.4: Alcohol as a portion of prevention research in Canada, 2005 - 2010. 0.33% as reported in the CCRA Survey.

Over the entire course of six years, seven PIs focused on alcohol in their research. If we imagine that they each had an equivalent grant, that would mean they each had $21,428.57 in each of their six years to spend on researching alcohol as a risk factor for cancer, slightly less than they would have received if they had each worked full-time at Taco Bell.

Most researchers would consider this amount of money "statistically negligible."

Is it because we have no patience for drunkards?

Dr. Christine Williams, Chief Mission Officer and Scientific Director at the Canadian Cancer Society (CCS) has some thoughts.

"Alcohol we know, definitively, is a carcinogen, but we don't talk about it and we don't connect research into it. IARC has shown that it is no doubt a carcinogen and CCS is just as quiet as anybody else about its associated risks. I've been badgering my staff that we need to do more on this. It's an education piece. Nothing has ever been as clear a carcinogen as tobacco, which has been effectively demonized. There's no mixed messaging. Alcohol is much more of a mixed message. Its role in cardiac protection is still being understood. But I do find it interesting how little investment there is in alcohol research and I should say, it's the same in other first world nations where it's part of the social culture."

The IARC study commented that alcohol beverages have a wide variety of functions for "humans." It's involved in "feasting and celebration." Sharing a drink can be a ritual for friendship or solidarity, the sealing of an agreement or a rite of passage. Alcohol, they also note, can also be associated with violence, disruption and addictions.

But its effectiveness as a moneymaker could be what seduces whole societies and governments into the willing arms of its favourite brand of hooch, no matter what the health effects.

The Canadian market in wine, beer and spirits is projected to grow to $42 billion in 2016. Consumption of alcohol throughout the world is growing.

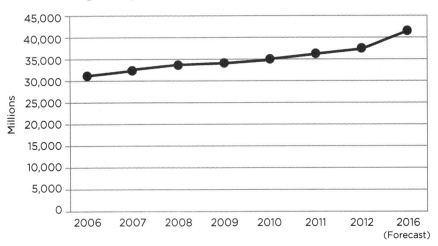

Figure 4.5: Canadian Market in Alcoholic Drinks.

The five cancers associated with alcohol as a risk factor are running at the head of the pack in terms of the predicted increased incidence of cancer in Canada over the next 15 years. The average annual new cases of oral cancer are predicted to increase by 60 per cent. Cancer of the esophagus, which killed celebrated writer, Christopher Hitchens in 2011, is expected to increase by 86.1 per cent. The number of people who contract colorectal cancer will increase by 78 per cent, liver cancer by 147.2 per cent and breast cancer by 55.4 per cent.

So if prevention research funding is not going into studies on contaminants in the air, water and soil, occupational exposures or alcohol as risk factors, then where is it going?

The largest percentage of prevention research funding in Canada is invested in Genetic Susceptibilities, studies that look at an individual's genetic make-up to see if there is predisposition to cancer, and from there, perhaps a method can be developed to prevent the cancer or set up the environment for an early diagnosis.

From 2005 to 2010, $50.7 million was invested in this area of prevention; research that connects with work being done at the molecular and genetic level in precision medicine. There were 88 PIs involved in genetic susceptibility research.

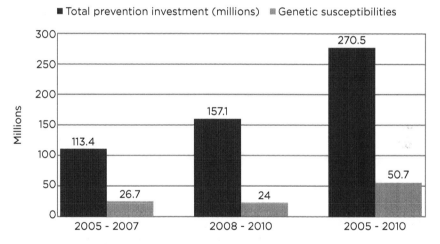

Figure 4.6: Genetic susceptibilities as a portion of prevention research in Canada, 2005 – 2010. 18.7% as reported in the CCRA Survey.

Health economist, Cindy Gauvreau, has some observations about personalized medicine, which she feels is still a long way away.

"To integrate personalized medicine into a standard of care that we can all accept is still very far away," she says, "because it has to be." "As for any new technology, there has to be acceptance, there has to be guidelines, and there has to be an infrastructure for it. And even apart from all that kind of stuff that's not in place yet, the other thing is the ethical part," she says.

And the ethical considerations of mapping genes to affect a cancer cure are significant. It may sound like a miracle cure—and clearly that is how it is being marketed by the charities raising hundreds of millions of dollars to conduct this expensive research—but the ethical issues around precision medicine border on the metaphysical.

Are genetic markers a predisposition for something or a certainty? With this technology, will we be setting the course of individual's life at birth? Does knowing an individual's genetic markers allow them to be segmented into a particular class of wellness from a very young age? Will genetic predisposition result in over-treatment? And, related to a more earthly concern, are insurance companies going to insist on seeing your genetic make-up prior to insuring you?

Despite the hundreds of millions of dollars being raised by charities in Canada to support personalized medicine, very little is being devoted to working through the ethics of this presumed advancement in cancer treatment, including an estimate of how many lives it may ultimately impact. This is a particularly relevant discussion in a world where only half the population can afford the HPV vaccine that is proven to prevent cervical cancer.

"As opposed to introducing a new cancer drug when we know some of the adverse affects from previous drugs, and where we have the structure, we have the pathway of treatment already; to treat at the genetic and molecular level is very, very far away."

"Maybe I'm wrong, but when I look at the infrastructure and how long it took us to get here…Cancer drugs were developed before the first world war and we're only now getting to the point where we are getting drugs with less toxicity."

Maybe the "long view" of prevention really isn't that long at all.

5/

Tax Incentives:
The Downside of Gratitude

Mr. Pearl Fisher is a fictional businessman/philanthropist living in a major city in Canada who wants to build the best, most acoustically pure and architecturally dazzling, audience-friendly opera house in the world.

People will come from all over to watch opera at this venue. Artists will book years in advance to appear there. And Mr. Fisher will foot the entire $3 billion cost of building the facility. He will hire the architect, buy the land from the city and choose the design. And, of course, he will have a charity set up to receive the money he donates.

How much will Mr. Pearl Fisher's $3 billion operatic dream actually cost him?

"There is no cap on how much charitable money you can give in Canada," says charity lawyer, Mark Blumberg. "If you have $10 billion and you want to give $1 billion to charity, you can. If you want to give $3 billion, you can. And if it's appreciable marketable securities, there could be up to sixty-five percent tax benefit."

So, if Mr. Fisher contributes $3 billion of appreciable marketable securities to the charity that's been registered to support his opera house, he will be eligible for a $1.95 billion tax credit. That is $1.95 billion cut right off the tally of Mr. Fisher's tax bill and $1.95 billion that doesn't come into the federal Treasury for spending on government priorities — perhaps even other arts initiatives.

Tax credits are the way in which the people of Canada say thank you to Mr. Fisher.

But Mr. Fisher hasn't seen the last of the return on his investment.

He is a businessman after all and one who is constantly on the look out for investors in his full range of global interests, which include mining, telecommunications, navigational technology and a new area of interest, renewable energy. How his potential investors perceive him is important. His brand is like cash to him. His reputation means money.

In order to build up his personal corporate brand he decides to name his opera house after himself in perpetuity. And why not? The Pearl Fisher Centre for the Performing Arts is being built on his nickel.

The Pearl Fisher Centre for the Performing Arts will become a global brand. His name will appear in all the right places, especially in that hard to reach "luxe" market, the one where Louis Vuitton, Fendi, Rolls Royce and Tiffany rule the day and where his prospective investors live. Opera will be broadcast from the Centre. Mr. Fisher can stand next to any opera singer he chooses. Cecilia Bartoli or Renée Fleming will be honoured to meet him. The conductors of the world's greatest orchestras will fete him too; performing artists of all stripes will be anxious to meet him. And they will be *grateful*.

You can't buy the kind of positive press coverage that The Pearl Fisher Centre for the Performing Arts will bring to Mr. Pearl Fisher's global reputation. Imagine the kind of people who will want to invest in his companies as a result of his re-vitalized personal brand. The $3 billion he invested (which, because of the tax credit, is already reduced to $1.05 billion) is nothing compared to the billions of dollars of investor money potentially coming his way. He feels good.

And even though you can't buy that kind of exposure, let's try to put a figure on it what it might be worth.

In 2012, Etihad Airways spent £400 million (CAD $780 million or USD $580 million) for a 10-year deal to sponsor Manchester City Football Club. Manchester City games are played in Etihad Stadium now and by sponsoring a football club, the airline jettisoned itself smack into the middle of the Euro psyche.

Branding experts say we are in the middle of "global naming rights explosion."

According to the *World Trademark Review,* a survey of sponsorship decision-makers around the world suggested the top motivating factors for naming rights are:

- Increasing awareness and visibility.
- Increasing brand loyalty.
- Changing or reinforcing corporate image.
- Showcasing community and social responsibility.
- Accessing a platform for experiential branding.

Also, the "number of media impressions a sponsorship receives is one of the driving forces behind the large amounts that companies are prepared to pay."

It turned out Mr. Pearl Fisher had put together a pretty savvy business deal. The naming rights, for 20 years at current market value (if we use the Etihad deal as a base)are worth CAD $1.56 billion, so if we add $1.95 billion in tax credits and the $1.56 billion in brand value, and subtract the $3 billion is cost to build the opera house, Mr. Fisher, after 20 years, has come out $510 million ahead on the deal.

He also has his opera house and numerous new investors for his own business interests. *And everyone is saying thank you.* They don't call him a smart businessman for nothing.

But, better still—maybe not for us but for him—is the absence of any public discussion of whether the city *needed* a world class opera house and whether the Canadian treasury *wanted* to fork over $1.95 billion in tax credits that the opera house charity had issued to Mr. Fisher.

When it comes to charities and how they spend their money, as long as it's legal, and no one is suggesting that anything Mr. Pearl Fisher did was illegal, there is nothing we can do. There is no recourse for the public in terms of how donations are prioritized.

The creation of endowments is another way donors have of direct-
ing large amounts of money to extend their belief system or area of
interest. A wealthy donor can make a contribution of $X million to
establish an endowment fund for a specific purpose. The condition
will be that the hospital foundation does not spend the principle and
must maintain its value. The donor will receive a tax receipt in the
year the donation is made and can claim the full value of the credit,
even though the donated funds themselves can never be spent.

Tennys Hanson, CEO of Toronto General & Western Hospital
Foundation, says the Foundation has 260 individual endowment
funds "supporting chairs, professorships, fellowships, lectureships,
awards and scholarships."

Tennys, a well-respected charity executive, has been with the
Toronto General & Western Hospital Foundation since 2000, was
the recipient of the Outstanding Fundraising Professional Award
Association of Fundraising Professionals in 2008.

"The majority of the funds we receive are directed by our donors
through specific agreements. We must honour these agreements,
receive and release the funds according to those agreements and
report back to our donors on an annual basis at minimum."

Toronto General says they pay out 3.5 per cent as investment
income from their endowments.

But do endowed funds make sense for a hospital, designed to
deal with acute care? Would anyone want an endowed fund to deal
with the Ebola virus or HIV/AIDS?

Endowed funds take money out of the economy, yet the tax
credit of up to 65 per cent means that the federal Treasury has *less*

money to spend on other health priorities and, as Tennys says, "the funds we receive are directed by our donors."

One wealthy person can build an opera house or set up an endowment fund and they have the right to decide where they want their money to go and that's how the charity world works. But what isn't so charitable is that the people of Canada don't have a say where funds are directed. As Tennys Hanson says, "it's up to the donor."

"That's what people don't get about tax receipts," says Mark Blumberg. "It's about real money not coming into the government coffers that other people have to pay more taxes to subsidize."

——•——

Imagine Canada is a lobby group for Canadian charities that has been petitioning for more tax incentives for many years. The most recent lobbying focus has been on what they've called the stretch credit, a credit that would incentivize larger gifts year over year. For example, if you gave $1,000 one year and $2,000 the next year, you would get your regular tax credit on the first thousand and a preferred tax rate on the second thousand.

Tax incentives are currently weighted in favour of people with higher taxable income. If, for example, a donor in Alberta with taxable income of $250,000, makes a cash donation of $20,000, he will receive a tax credit of $10,742. If that donor had a taxable income of $100,000, the tax credit would be worth $9,950. That's the way the Canadian charitable tax credit system is set up. The more money you make, the greater your charitable tax credit.

"It seems that the one thing the sector agrees on is that when wealthy people donate to charity, they should be given souped-up tax credits," says Mark Blumberg. "But why should it cost a wealthy person, say a billionaire, only thirty-five cents on the dollar when they give to charity by appreciated market securities, but an average person who gives to charity may be getting no tax incentive at all."

Fundraising guru, Ken Wyman, has the same misgivings with regard to the focus on incentivizing tax credits. With more than 35 years' experience in the nonprofit sector, Ken has raised millions of dollars and contributed to eight books on fundraising. Ken also led the full-time post-graduate certificate program at Humber College for twelve years.

"Canada already has the most generous tax incentives for charitable giving in the world," Ken says. "Imagine Canada's full focus for advocacy over the last few years has been on more and better tax breaks, and changing the tax breaks on capital gains and stretch tax credits. This opens the door to further reasons why major givers, who are already tremendously influential, to become more influential."

"I would say there's a misunderstanding of our tactical approach," says Bruce MacDonald, Imagine Canada's CEO. "The tax incentive that we championed (it's been a five-year effort) was actually aimed at the masses, not at the elite."

He says that while they were working to get the stretch tax credit included in the 2016 federal budget, there was an initiative for a capital gains exemption on the sale of land and company shares when cash proceeds from the disposition of private corporation shares or real estate are donated to a registered charity or other qualified donee within 30 days.

"[The capital gains exemption] was not championed by us," he says, "but we did indicate our support. We were championing the stretch. And when asked by government the difference between the two, the case that we were trying to make was that the stretch was for every Canadian regardless of income level."

Bruce says Imagine Canada felt the conservative government of the day was not interested in a macro-level conversation about social good, and that the tax credit incentive instrument mirrored their style of enacting public policy through boutique tax credits. He says Imagine Canada was adapting its style to the government.

"If boutique tax credits were going to become the vehicle through which public policy was going to be delivered, then we had to get in the game or sit it out."

The newly elected Liberal government did not adopt the Imagine Canada Stretch Tax Credit in its 2016 budget. Nor did it move ahead with an enhanced capital gains credit for donations made after the sale of private company shares and real estate.

"Had the bottom not fallen out of oil prices, I think we would have had [the stretch tax credit]," Bruce MacDonald says. "If you go back to the ideology of the Conservative government, this fit very nicely, because, unlike some of the other tax credits that had been implemented over the last number of years, this was going to benefit Canadians in any one of their constituencies, regardless of economic wealth."

"It was 'the people's' tax credit."

———

The charitable sector has been a battleground, and possibly collateral damage, in the fight for reduced taxes and reduced government spending.

The clash is between the idea of paying taxes and making donations.

The consequence of an individual paying taxes is that you give money to government who spends it on things based on the desire of the voters.

The consequence of an individual donor making a donation to charity is that the donation is given to the donor's area of interest. Then, depending on the amount of the donation and the taxable income of the donor, up to 65 per cent of the donation amount will be credited back to the donor. The donor pays less tax as a result of supporting her personal cause and revenue is diverted from the federal Treasury.

Yet, despite the fact that Canadian taxpayers are paying for tax credits, there is no obligation on the part of the charity that is issuing the tax credit to be working on behalf of the common good. A charity's mandate is to work on behalf of the people under its umbrella.

"In 2014, $15.7 billion in tax receipts were issued, but just over $8 billion was claimed," says Mark Blumberg. "Six billion was not even claimed on tax returns."

He believes that it is the people contributing less money to charity who are not claiming the credit.

"If you talk to anyone on Bay Street or you talk to someone who advises the wealthy, that's an anathema to them," Mark says. "So when one looks at the $8 billion that was claimed, it's a disproportionately large number of wealthy donors who are taking advantage of the tax credit because if their accountant didn't put the receipt on the tax return, they'd get fired—and sued."

Many donors, even wealthy donors, are not necessarily motivated by tax credits. The problem with the current tax incentive system is that it tends to do a better job of incentivizing wealthy people to put money into their pet projects as opposed to funding areas of greatest need.

And gratitude is the default state of mind.

6/

How Can You Compete with People Who Are Changing the Skyline?

The advertising campaign launched on behalf of Toronto's Sick Kids Hospital in late 2014 blew people's minds.

The Sick Kids Foundation's vice president of brand marketing and communications, David Estok and his team joined up with the Foundation's longtime ad agency, JWT, to create *Better Tomorrows,* a campaign comprised of 45 different documentary style spots that featured children undergoing treatment at the hospital for life-threatening illnesses.

One story was about little Charlize.

Charlize's spot opens with a shot of an official looking "Discharge Check DisC" label, then pans over to a close up of the nametag on her bed. There's a hand-drawn heart in front of her name. The camera pans to her stuffed toys and ultimately settles on Charlize's sweet face. There were no tubes or other medical accessories attached to her body that could obscure the beauty of this infant. The soft piano chords of Coldplay's anthem, *Fix You,* are introduced to the audio as the camera zooms in on Charlize for a super close-up.

Coldplay's frontman, Chris Martin wrote the song *Fix You* for his then future wife Gwyneth Paltrow when she was devastated by the loss of her father, Bruce Paltrow. Chris and Gwyneth ended up marrying in 2003, having two children, Apple and Moses, and then famously "consciously uncoupled" in 2014.

The song is an ode to the helplessness and longing we share when we are trying to help someone we love.

As the piano chords of the song become more recognizable, a woman, presumably Charlize's mother, leans in to gently pick the baby's head up off the mattress and kisses her lovingly on the fore-head. She murmurs "Hello, Charlie bear."

Words appear across the middle of the screen.

"She was born with a rare heart condition."

As mom lays the baby back down on her bed, another sentence appears.

"And she needed two open-heart surgeries to survive."

The camera pans over Charlize again. She is nestled in pastel pink blankets but her neck and chest, completely free of medical devices, are uncovered, fully exposed to the camera, the personification of vulnerability. The piano continues and Martin begins to softly sing the famous chorus.

"And I will—"

But Chris Martin's vocals get cut before he gets to the "try-y-y-y-y to fix you" part of the line the audio is replaced with the mechanical beeping sounds of a typical hospital room. The words on the screen change again.

"When a child is diagnosed with an illness, their entire life is put on pause."

Little Charlize is then shown in a freeze frame. Her eyes are closed. Her chest is still bare. There is no movement at all. No breathing. No fluttering of eyelids. The only sound you can hear on the audio is the beep-beep-beep of a heart monitor. What has happened to this child?

New words appear.

"Because of your donations, together we helped to unpause Charlize's story."

More hospital noises are brought onto the soundtrack and the scene abruptly changes.

As the full orchestral chorus of the Coldplay song begins to swell, a sweet little dynamo of a baby in a navy blue flowered jumper and pink leggings appears on screen taking the corner around a living room couch on all fours, but with considerable speed. She's wearing the cutest little, "I had you guys going, didn't I?" smile.

More words appear on the screen.

"This year she's finally home—"

And get this…

"—looking strong and healthy like her *twin sister*," who then comes running into the shot. She is identical to and wearing the same outfit as little Charlize!

We see a close-up of Charlize's hands and face, a shot of her face through the rails of the stairs and of her crawling, joyfully, into her mother's lap.

"Another life unpaused," say the words on the screen.

"Another life unpaused, thanks to you."

Chris Martin's voice sings out now.

"Lights will guide you home /And I will try to fix you."

Charlize stands up next to her mother who is thrilled and says, "Good job, pumpkin! Good job!"

Boom!

If you like that, there are 44 more just like it.

———

"We wanted to do something that would juxtapose what was going on in [the consumer's] life," Dave Estok told *Strategy* magazine in November 2014.

"If you're having a bad day, you might see one of these and realize someone who is three years old has cancer and is having surgery today. Over the course of 45 days, we can convey a wide variety of emotions."

Estok told the magazine that as with many philanthropic organizations, Sick Kids' holiday push is its most important, as donations from this time of year represents roughly 25 per cent of the foundation's annual budget.

Mindshare, an international media-buying agency, handled the buy on the campaign and the foundation was able to get three spots donated for every one that it bought.

Donations would be made online and would serve to strength the Foundation's digital presence.

Reports in *Strategy* magazine indicated the *Better Tomorrows* campaign achieved a "one-month donation record of $37 million in December 2014 (23 per cent higher than the previous record)" and "the campaign drove a 13 per cent propensity to donate."

The videos had more 560,000 views on YouTube. The Foundation garnered 8,000 new Facebook followers, a 7 per cent increase.

The campaign won a Silver Lion at Cannes among several other industry awards and accolades.

Fast forward to the spring of 2015.

In March, David Estok, whose already impressive *bona fides* now buoyed by the unprecedented success of the JWT-directed *Better Tomorrows* campaign is headed over to the University of Toronto to become their new vice president of communications.

Throughout his career, David has swung between the newspaper business and nonprofit sector. He began his career as a journalist at the *Hamilton Spectator*, a newspaper founded in 1846 in a southwestern Ontario town best known for its steel production and Canadian Football League team, the Hamilton Tiger Cats. He spent three years at *The Financial Post* as a senior editor, a year as business editor at *Macleans* magazine and ten years as associate vice president of communications and public affairs at Western University in London, Ontario. When he arrived at Sick Kids in 2010, he'd just finished a three-year stint as editor-in-chief of his old newspaper, the *Hamilton Spectator*. Now, in the spring of 2015, he was off to the University of Toronto on a new adventure as one of the most senior — and well-paid — executives in the entire charitable sector.

By May, Lori Davison, who had come to the Sick Kids Foundation directly from Leo Burnett Toronto in late summer 2014 — and had spent a year under David Estok as his director of branding and communications — replaced him as VP of brand marketing and communications. Prior to Leo Burnett, Lori had worked at BBDO for six years. During her seven-year ad agency stint, her accounts included the Government of Ontario, RBC and TD Bank.

But what did JWT get for the trouble of taking their client on a winning road to Cannes along with precedent-setting fundraising records?

The Sick Kids Foundation put their advertising business out to tender.

At the end of May, it was announced that Cossette, headquartered in Quebec City, had won the pitch and became the Sick Kids Foundation's new agency of record. At the same time, it was stated that OMD Worldwide would take over the media buying from Mindshare.

"In both cases, we were inspired by the insights brought forward as well as their demonstration of passion for our cause," Lori Davison said in a written statement. "This is an important milestone in our journey to the next campaign and with these exceptional partners in place we are poised to accomplish great things."

JWT had declined to pitch for renewed business on the Sick Kids account, which they had worked on since 2003.

All the same, Sick Kids couldn't depart too far from the winning formula set up by JWT's *Better Tomorrows* campaign.

"We came away with this incredibly rich body of content — some of which had only appeared once in the world," Lori Davison told *Strategy* magazine. "We saw this next campaign as an opportunity to keep telling those stories."

The *Life on Pause* campaign was born.

Peter Ignazi, chief creative officer at Cossette said, "Our insight from the brief was that when a kid is going through the process of being in the hospital, their lives are put on hold. They're on pause. And so are the families."

The *Life on Pause* campaign would re-visit six of the children it had featured in the *Better Tomorrows* campaign, the ones who were able to return to normal lives after their treatment at Sick Kids, to see how they were faring one year later.

But a new element would be introduced into the campaign. Viewers would have to make a donation to "unlock" the ending and be able to see how things turned out for the child featured in each spot. Fundraising goals were set to each child's story.

One story was about a little boy, Kael, who looks to be about two or three. It's hard to tell. As the video opens, he is half crying, half whimpering, seemly without enough strength to do either. His little face is bloated and he looks somewhat jaundiced. It's not clear whether it's from the disease or the medication. He has an NG tube (nasogastric tube) used for administering medication or feeding tucked up into his nostril and taped to his face. We are told Kael has a rare immune disorder. There's another shot of him with little weights in his hand trying to play a game with his dad, where he's straining to lift the weights and "punch" his dad's palms. Then the frame freezes.

In order to "unpause" Kael's story, to find out how things turned out, a certain number of donations would have to be made. In this case the number of donations was matched with the number of nights Kael spent in hospital — 440.

Charlize, one of the six stories featured in 2015, could only have her story "unlocked" after 707 people went online and donated. The number 707 was targeted to "unlock" her story because her family lives 707 kilometers from the hospital.

Through a donation, the donor could virtually "unpause" the life of a sick child. And the idea of needing more than one would (theoretically, at least) encourage people to use their social media networks to make sure enough donations were made to "unlock" the child's ending.

"Our challenge is less about marketing and more about the overall state of giving," Lori Davison told *Media in Canada*. "The pie is shrinking, so for us the challenge is to always try to grow our giving within a shrinking environment."

The print campaign showed pictures of Kael, Charlize and four other seriously ill children named Taylum, Gabriel, Liam and Finlay with the word PAUSED superimposed over their faces.

Accolades from the advertising industry and media commentators continued to pour in.

University Avenue is Toronto's grand boulevard. At the northern end, surrounded by landscaped gardens and made of pink-hued sandstone that sparkles on a sunny day, stands Ontario's Legislative Building, Queen's Park. Named for Queen Victoria and opened in 1860, it was designated the "pink place" when the left of centre New Democrats were in power from 1990 to 1995. It is set on higher ground within an oval park, also called Queen's Park. Looking south towards Lake Ontario, three lanes of traffic in each direction and a landscaped median featuring memorial statues, foundations and gardens unroll in front of you. The subway runs underneath University Avenue and will take you to Union Station. Union Station will take you to pretty nearly anywhere in the world.

The distance between Queen's Park Subway Station and the next stop, Saint Patrick Subway Station, is .6 km or .37 miles. The ride takes two minutes underground. The walk takes about nine minutes above ground.

On the right are two acute care hospitals—Princess Margaret Cancer Hospital (610 University Avenue) and Mount Sinai Hospital (600 University Avenue). Underneath the Mount Sinai sign the small print reads Joseph and Wolf Lebovic Health Complex. The block-long boarding that envelopes Princess Margaret Cancer Hospital rings out with the message that "Cancer Can Be Cured in Your Lifetime."

The emergency entrance to Mount Sinai Hospital is designated as the Schwartz/Reisman Emergency Centre. It, too, is undergoing massive renovation.

Across the street are two more acute care hospitals, Toronto General Hospital (University and Gerrard) and Sick Kids Hospital (555 University Avenue). During the holiday season, when the Santa Claus parade marches down the avenue and the buildings are lit up for the celebration, the lights on Sick Kids Hospital feature a bear with a bandage on his head driving a train that looks like *The Little Engine that Could*.

The hospitals are just south of the MaRS Discovery Centre, an "innovation hub" that was set up to house companies who could potentially commercialize publicly-funded medical research.

This part of University Avenue is sometimes called "Hospital Row." It's not hard to imagine a cloud of winged dollar bills zooming like snitches, Quidditch-style, out of the coffers of Queen's Park right into hospital boiler rooms.

In addition to provincial government funding, each hospital has its own fundraising foundation, their own donors and their own fundraising staff. The combined assets of the four foundations are $2.21 billion and are made up of investments in Canadian, U.S. and foreign equities, bonds, currency, hedge funds, mortgages funds and private capital pooled funds.

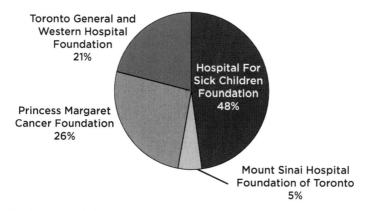

Figure 6.1: Asset breakdown by hospital, 2015. ($2.21 Billion)

The value of the assets held by these four charitable foundations has grown by 226 per cent since 2006.

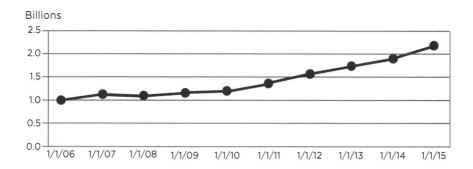

Date	Assets
2006-01-01	$977,683,880
2007-01-01	$1,097,714,522
2008-01-01	$1,082,032,677
2009-01-01	$1,139,166,476
2010-01-01	$1,201,163,984
2011-01-01	$1,421,239,711
2012-01-01	$1,560,279,305
2013-01-01	$1,736,580,038
2014-01-01	$1,934,570,731
2015-01-01	$2,212,674,283

Figure 6.2: Asset growth from 2006-2015 ($2.21 billion).

The assets are, by and large, donor-driven says Tennys Hanson, CEO of the Toronto General and Western Hospital Foundation (TGWHF) and made up of donor-directed endowment funds that pay out at 3.5 per cent a year.

"The endowment funds are directed by donors through specific agreements," she says.

CEO of Sick Kids Foundation, Ted Garrard, says that, "it is important to note that most of the assets in the endowment are restricted by the donor as per the use of the funds and we are only able to pay out earnings on these funds, not encroach on the capital."

Sick Kids Foundation has a payout policy of 4.5 per cent on endowments, Ted says, and any additional investment revenue is not spent, but added back to the capital.

All but one year of Ted's career, when he acted as Ontario Liberal Policy Research Officer, has been spent in the charity sector. He did a stint at the United Way of Greater Toronto and spent 13 years as the chief fundraiser, the Vice-President External, at the University

6/ How Can You Compete with People Who Are Changing the Skyline?

of Western Ontario and was the 1997 recipient of the National Society of Fundraising Executive Toronto Chapter's *Outstanding Fundraising Executive* Award.

"We don't apologize for having endowments," he says. "They are an important source of stable revenue for the hospital. They are a means by which donors can perpetuate their charitable intentions after their deaths and we feel we have been very good stewards of those endowments."

Not all of the four hospital foundations are saving, raising and spending money at the same rate. 75 per cent of the $2.21 billion in assets belong to Princess Margaret Cancer Foundation and the Sick Kids Hospital Foundation.

Kevin Goldthorp, CEO of the Mount Sinai Foundation, whose Foundation accounted for the smallest slice of Hospital Row assets (at 5 per cent) says, "there needs to be balance, everything in moderation. We have some endowment coming off and we have restricted cash we're holding for projects and for us now that's $20 million."

"We try to move the money through the Foundation pretty quickly at Mount Sinai."

There is no word on Princess Margaret Cancer Foundation's position on its asset policy. Paul Alofs, the Foundation's CEO, declined to be interviewed for this book.

—·—

Between 2006 and 2015, four hospital foundations built up $2.21 billion in primarily donor-directed assets, raised a combined $4.50 billion in annual revenue and had $3.50 billion in expenditures, $1.07 billion of which was on advertising, promotion and fundraising, more than was spent on all three federal elections held during that time period.

	Hospital for Sick Children Foundation	Mount Sinai Hospital Foundation of Toronto	Princess Margaret Cancer Foundation	Toronto General & Western Hospital Foundation	Totals
Money spent on advertising & promotion	$92,125,211	$18,882,202	$90,281,120	$15,452,168	$216,740,701
Money spent on fundraising	$387,951,447	$46,545,443	$317,046,778	$98,850,400	$850,394,068
Fundraising revenue	$1,121,365,836	$373,812,638	$1,132,541,150	$656,029,802	$3,283,749,426
Percentage of fundraising expenditures over fundraising revenue	34.6%	12.5%	28.0%	15.1%	25.9%
Total revenue from all sources	$1,657,229,790	$432,196,469	$1,539,281,553	$850,342,959	$4,479,050,771
Percentage of fundraising revenue as overall revenue	64.4%	99.2%	74.8%	77.7%	73.5%
Total expenditures	$1,257,778,158	$381,906,427	$1,254,147,496	$556,015,997	$3,449,848,078
Percentage revenue over expenditures	131.8%	113.2%	122.7%	152.9%	129.8%

FR + Promotion: **$1,067,134,769**
Revenue over expenses: **$1,029,202,693**

Figure 6.3: Hospital row foundations financial snapshot, 2006-2015.

That amount is double what a comparative sampling of Canada's most well-known charitable brands such as Canadian Red Cross or CNIB spends and quadruple what is spent by a combined sampling of Canada's most well- known cancer charities such as the Canadian Cancer Society or the Canadian Breast Cancer Foundation.

The questions are: Why are hospital foundations fundraising

so aggressively when hospital operations are primarily funded by government and why are they not spending the money they *are* raising?

Kevin Goldthorp of Mount Sinai underlines the cost of doing business in the brutally competitive world of medical research.

Like Ted Garrard, Kevin Goldthorp has a background at the University of Western Ontario. He actually took over from Ted Garrard as the new Vice-President, External, when Ted left the university to work at the Sick Kids Foundation and led the re-branding strategy that culminated with the university undergoing a name change to Western University. He is familiar with the dynamics of health sector fundraising. Prior to joining Mount Sinai, he spent six years as Chief Executive Officer of the Sunnybrook Hospital Foundation.

He was justifiably excited the day we met because *The Brain Prize* had just been awarded to Dr. Graham Collingridge, one of the hospital's recent all-star recruits from Bristol, U.K. A hugely prestigious award, *The Brain Prize* is given to "one or more scientists who have distinguished themselves by making an outstanding contribution to European neuroscience and who are still active in research." The Prize carries with it a €1 million (CAD $1.46 million or USD $1.13 million) personal award for the researcher.

"Foundations are raising more than they are spending because they're raising money for chair endowments that fund a researcher or a clinical positions," Kevin says. "These positions are precarious. What happens if you don't have the money to pay a researcher's salary? Are you supposed to say, 'You aren't getting paid this month?' Is doesn't work like that."

But isn't that what happens in other charities when they don't have the money?

"It doesn't work in an international marketplace," says Kevin

Goldthorp. "Think about the intellectual capital you require for a hospital. You are hiring people who can go anywhere in the world and they have offers from around the world."

"If you're hiring someone in another charity to do social service or other work, there's much more fluidity in that job market."

The amount of money spent on fundraising by major hospital foundations is staggeringly high in relation to most other charities.

The stratified nature of the sector is reflected in the average wages and the percentage of part-time work. A large hospital foundation has an average staff salary of $102,000. Staff in a community-based charity earn an average of $25,000. The percentage of part-time workers increases the further you go down the charity food chain.

Charity segment	Average wage	Hourly wage for a 37.5 hour week	Part time workers	Full time workers
Hospital row	$102,179.25	$52.40	10.49%	89.51%
Cancer fundraising organizations (members of CCRA)	$69,098.59	$35.44	21.98%	78.02%
International Non-Governmental Organizations	$50,874.73	$26.09	26.69%	73.31%
Canadian average wage	$48,964.50	$25.11	19.28%	80.72%
Recognized non-cancer charitable brands	$38,809.72	$19.90	44.02%	55.98%
Community organizations	$25,035.16	$12.84	55.03%	44.97%

Figure 6.4: Charity compensation comparison.

Canadian charities, like charities around the world, are structured like sedimentary rock, each layer representing the wealth, status and standing of the charity. People who have the money, spend the money to make more money. The ability of wealthy charities to outspend their competition allows them to define the priorities of the sector, entrenching the systemic inequity that exists in society at large.

Such is the power of advertising that most donors would likely say that the level of patient care delivered at Sick Kids Hospital, for example, is reliant on support from charitable donations.

Bruce MacDonald, CEO of Imagine Canada, the sector's de facto lobby group, bristled at the idea of donations to the Sick Kids Hospital Foundation not supporting patient care.

"You're suggesting that *no* money raised by the Sick Kids Foundation is supporting patient care at the hospital?" he asked with skepticism.

"We don't support direct patient care," says Ted Garrard, CEO of Sick Kids Hospital Foundation.

"Seventeen per cent of the $103.5 million ($17.6 million) given to the hospital went to patient-related programs such as pet therapy, music therapy, therapeutic clowns, financial assistance for patient families that need help with things like transit or parking support and capital projects that have a patient-related impact."

Similarly, Toronto General and Western Hospital Foundation devoted only 8 per cent ($5.5 million) of its funding to patient care in 2015.

"Most people in the public don't understand the way in which hospitals are funded or the constraints under which hospitals are being funded today or fully appreciate the cost of actually running a world class health care institution," says Ted Garrard.

"Quite frankly, the cost to government to replace what philanthropy is doing would be prohibitive and, in fact, would increase taxes. The ROI that the public is getting through charitable tax credits is far greater than the cost of being able to provide those credits."

―――

The reality of life in large hospital foundations is that the vast majority of money they raise goes into research.

- 69% ($45.0 million) of funding raised by Toronto General and Western Hospital Foundation was devoted to research.
- 77% of the $103.5 of funding the Sick Kids Foundation provided to the hospital went to research.

And, as Kevin Goldthorp at Mount Sinai points out, health care research is a globally competitive environment, where the goal is to lure the world's top researchers to your hospital. The bigger your name, the more money you can raise. It's like bringing a great starting pitcher to a baseball team and star researchers, just like big-league starting pitchers, don't come cheap.

"Toronto & Western General Hospital are global leaders in terms of the global research work we do," says Tennys Hanson. "Patient care would not be where it is today without philanthropic support for research."

The Sick Kids Hospital audit provides an idea of the financial instruments used to supply money to medical research. Here are excerpts from the hospital's 2015 audit notes detailing how the research funds flow:

- At March 31, 2015, the Foundation holds $1.075 billion [2014 - $948.9 million] in unrestricted, restricted and endowment funds to be used primarily to support research, educational activities and capital investments at the Hospital.
- The Foundation granted $103.5 million [2014 - $125.1 million] to the Hospital for research, education, capital and debenture operating interest expense. These grants are recorded as revenue, deferred contributions or deferred capital contributions in the Hospital's financial statements.
- In 2009, associated with the construction of the Peter Gilgan Centre for Research and Learning, the Hospital issued Debentures. The Debentures bear interest at 5.217 % which is payable semi-annually on June 16 and December 16 with the principal amount to be repaid on December 16, 2049.
- Concurrent with the issuance of the Debentures, the Hospital entered into two funding agreements with the Foundation, the Research Tower Funding Agreement and the Core Funding Agreement. The Research Tower Funding Agreement provided for the conduct [of] a capital fundraising campaign in respect of the Peter Gilgan Centre for Research and Learning.
- In general, the Foundation's grants under the Research Tower Funding Agreement took precedence over any other commitments of the Foundation to the Hospital. The Hospital used a portion of the grants toward the design and construction costs of the Peter Gilgan Centre for Research and Learning and a portion to support the Hospital's interest and principal obligations related to the Debentures.

A debenture is a bond issued by an institution that is looking to raise private money for a specific project. Issuing debentures is like putting a page up on a crowd sourcing website like Kickstarter and asking people for money to support your work. But with a debenture, you'd be asking people for a loan not a straight up gift.

The people who are crowd-sourcing your loan feel confident enough in your reputation that they don't need to have the loan secured by collateral. A debenture is secured based on your good reputation. Your second-hand Honda Civic, for example, is safe. Instead of the project having to abide by the regulations of Kickstarter, issuing debentures means you have to comply with the rules of the securities regulator in your province.

Your Kickstarter buddy will pay you interest on the amount of money you've lent to his project until the time he has to repay the loan (debenture) in full.

In the case of the Sick Children's Hospital, the Board of Trustees of the Hospital decided they needed to build a world-class research centre.

Obviously, world-class research centres takes mega-bucks to build so they need to get a loan or "raise capital" for the building. The hospital decided to do their version of a KickStarter campaign and let the bond market know they would be issuing $200 million of debentures. The debentures would "bear interest at 5.217 per cent which is payable semi-annually on June 16 and December 16 with the principal amount to be repaid on December 16, 2049."

So if you invest in stocks and bonds, and you see the Sick Kids Hospital offering up a debenture, you're thinking, hey, that's a pretty safe bet and I could do worse than 5.217 per cent, so you buy $100,000 in Sick Kids debentures. That means, every six months you'll get an interest payment on your debenture along with the promise to repay your $100,000 by 2049.

According to the hospital's audit, "for the year ended March 31, 2015, interest payable to [debenture] bondholders was $10.4 million" and according to the terms of the Research Tower Funding Agreement, the foundation is supporting the "Hospital's interest and principal obligations related to the Debentures."

So we know that of the $103.5 million given to the hospital by the Foundation, $10.4 million of that, almost exactly ten cents on the dollar, went to paying off the interest on the debentures.

The decision to build a world-class research centre was *not* a matter for public consultation or discussion. Research priorities at Sick Kids are like the priorities of any charity. The board directors represent the line of public accountability and they determine priorities. The board is elected by the membership. Members are sometimes compared to shareholders, but the definition of a member in a charitable organization, found in the bylaws, can differ among charities and it is up to the discretion of the board.

The Board of Trustees for Sick Kids Hospital includes six members of the executive suite of banking or wealth management, six CEOs of transnational corporations, two CEOs of domestic corporations, two senior executives in biotechnology and two public sector CEOs.

"Most of the boards in Canada are constituted in the same way," says Ted Garrard, "and they are getting subsidies from government too."

The advance billing for The Peter Gilgan Research Centre touted it as an "architectural landmark" on University Avenue. The 21-storey $400 million tower of research space is said to be the "largest child health research tower in the world" and is home for 2,000 employees who had previously been housed in six separate locations.

The build was financed by $200 million of debentures and a capital campaign for $200 million. The capital campaign was financed with a contribution of more than $100 million by all three levels of government, as well as the Canada Foundation for Innovation, and lead donor, developer Peter Gilgan, whose $40 million dollars was enough to have the facility—which faces onto Bay Street—named after him. Peter Gilgan, CEO and Chairman of Mattamy Homes, is Canada's largest homebuilder. Forbes reports his net worth at $2.2 billion (#21 in Canada).

The Research Centre had close to $200 million in revenue last year, revenue that's part of Sick Kids Hospital overall budget. It received $125.8 million in research grants and awards, $122.3 million (97.3 per cent) of which was from government agencies, such as the Canadian Institute for Health Research (CIHR). The Sick Kids Foundation contributed another $61 million.

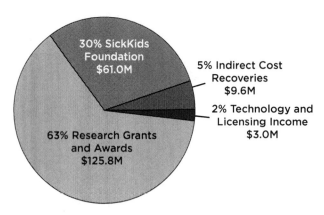

Figure 6.5a: Sources of funding for the Peter Gilgan Research Centre 2014—2015 ($199.5 million).

$33.3M	Canadian Institutes of Health Research
$21.4M	Canada Foundation for Innovation
$12.4M	Genome Canada
$9.7M	Ministry of Research and Innovation
$8.9M	Canada Research Chairs Program
$7.1M	National Institutes of Health
$2.0M	Ontario Brain Institute
$1.9M	Ontario Institute for Cancer Research
$1.5M	Natural Sciences and Engineering Research Council of Canada
$1.3M	JDRF Canadian Clinical Trial Network
$1.2M	Canadian Cancer Society
$1.0M	Terry Fox Research Institute

Figure 6.5b: Sources of research grants and awards of over $1M for the Peter Gilgan Research Centre 2014–2015 ($101.7 million).

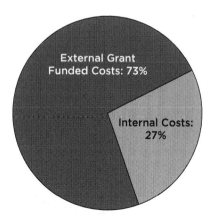

Figure 6.5c: Peter Gilgan Research Centre Expenditure, Internal vs. External, 2014–2015 ($214.5 million).

19%	Scientist salaries
18%	Bondholder expenses
18%	Depreciation
18%	Research operations
11%	Start-ups and bridge funding
8%	Scientific support
7%	Rent, Building and Core Facilities
4%	PGCRL Operations

Figure 6.5d: Peter Gilgan Research Centre Internal Expenditure Breakdown 2014—2015 ($57.9 million).

The amount of money spent on health care in Canada is enormous.

Total health care expenditures made by the federal government in 2015 reached almost $220 billion with 60 per cent of that going into hospitals, drugs and physicians. By comparison 5.5 per cent goes towards public health funding that focuses on prevention and wellness.

In the 2016/17 provincial budget, health care spending was projected at 40 per cent ($50.8 billion) of the entire budget in Ontario, 38 per cent ($18.0 billion) in British Columbia and 40 per cent ($20.4 billion) in Alberta.

With 40 per cent of provincial budgets devoted towards health care and hospital foundations raising hundreds of millions of tax-creditable dollars a year for bio-medical research, I asked Ted Garrard what amount of money hospitals would need in order to say they have enough.

"I don't think I can give you a number," he said. "I think it goes back to the question of the quality of life. What kind of quality of life do we want as Ontarians, as Canadians and what are we prepared to pay to get that quality of life? I would argue that putting money against healthcare is also really backstopping, if you will, a productive society. If we have an unhealthy society, an educated society, you aren't going to be able to keep the economy moving as it should. So there is no particular number."

7 /

The Next Best Thing

Brock Warner would, if he could, make himself invisible.

He is 30-years-old and, as a development manager, raises money for War Child Canada. He wants the attention to be focused on people half a world away.

War Child is an international charity that acts with local partners to provide education and support in areas torn apart by war. Compared to big players like World Vision, Plan Canada and Save the Children, War Child is small. Brock says that "makes them nimble" and they can go places other groups choose not to go.

"If other groups with more resources wanted to come and work in the areas we work in, I think we'd be happy to go to the other places people don't go. But, there's very few groups working in the areas War Child is in," he says.

From the start of his career, people have noticed Brock's talent. He is empathetic, smart and tends to see things in their "context," as he says, not only looking at the challenge that lies in front of him, but bringing in all the external factors that have a bearing on that problem.

He's involved with fundraising because he believes in human rights and social action.

Brock has studied his craft. He's done a year-long post-secondary diploma in Fundraising & Volunteer Management at Humber College in Toronto, database courses and is a CFRE (Certified Fund Raising Executive), an international designation to indicate he has passed an exam to administered by the sector's self-regulating body, the Association of Fundraising Professionals (AFP).

"I like solving problems and trying new things," says Brock, "and I find the harder thing is often the right thing. Bigger shops aren't as nimble. We need to try to be really clever with how we find new constituencies. If War Child can be at the leading edge of new technologies and new strategies, we can go in, have fun and set some examples, do some case studies, get some new donors and, most importantly, get the work done."

In 2014, Brock was enjoying his work at War Child but he also had itchy feet.

After three years, the fact that he hadn't yet gone into the field was starting to niggle at him. If it didn't happen soon, he was prepared to start looking around for other opportunities. If he was going to do his best work, he felt he needed to see War Child's impact first-hand on the ground.

"I wanted to see where the money I've been helping to raise was going. International development is not like a food bank or a shelter where your office is where the mission is," he says. "And for War Child, it's even further than most. INGOs (International Non-Governmental Organizations) who make long-term commitments to building projects, like Oxfam, or peace-building projects with women can go and visit them regularly. But the nature of War Child's work is that it's in areas that are difficult to work in. If there was easier access, I suspect we'd see the better-equipped and more well-funded organizations working there."

In 2014, an opportunity came up. One of the first funders of War Child's work in the Democratic Republic of Congo (DRC) wanted to go there and Brock could be part of that trip. There were some logistical problems. They'd have to stay in Burundi and cross the border every day, but they figured that could be managed. Plans were made, MOUs were signed, logistics put together. Then, in April, the Ebola outbreak happened in North Africa and, even through the DRC was nowhere near the outbreak, all travel to Africa was called off by the funder.

A few months later, in early 2015, another opportunity came

up—and it came up quickly.

"Do you want to go to South Sudan?" Brock was asked.

"Yeah, of course I do," was his reply.

"Next month?"

"Okay, next month."

South Sudan is the product of 50 years of war that had, in various iterations, varying slices of enemies in conflict. There was civil war between north and south, ethnic violence between the Dinka and Nuer peoples, religious strife when strident Islamists came close to power. Since 1956, after Sudan became independent of British and Egyptian colonial rule, more than two million people have died in conflict situations. Sudan was practically a synonym for war torn. The country and its troubles entered the consciousness of many North Americans when actor, George Clooney, made it his personal mission to do what he could, and travelled there extensively, developing relationships with politicians and the media, to try to bring attention to the conflicts.

In 2011, Sudan formally split into Sudan and South Sudan. The decision was made by referendum with a 98 per cent turnout in South Sudan and the South Sudanese people decided to go it alone. Juba was declared the capital city. But internecine violence continued.

Then, in December 2013, South Sudan exploded. There was an attempted coup in Juba, reportedly by ethnic Nuers, against the president, Salva Kiir, a Dinka. Riek Machar, the Nuer leader fled from Juba and set up a command post in the north of South Sudan. Ethnic violence enveloped the country.

Investigative journalist, Alex Perry, has written about Africa, in particular Sudan, for many years and for several publications. He covered one trip George Clooney had made in October, 2014 for *Newsweek*.

In that article, *George Clooney, South Sudan and How the World's Newest Nation Imploded*, he wrote the following:

"[In December 2013] Nuer and Dinka mobs began attacking their neighbours. Militias went house to house, demanding to know who was Nuer, who Dinka. Thousands were executed, their bodies left in the street. Children were shot as they ran. Fathers had their throats cut in front of their families. Women and girls were abducted and raped…As in Rwanda, families turned on each other. Women and children who sought safety in churches and hospitals and schools and outside UN bases were slaughtered en masse. When a Nuer militia fell on the northern town of Bentiu, massacring hundreds on April 15th and 16th, the UN reported that the killers were spurred on by exhortations on local radio stations, just as they had been in Rwanda."

Figure 7.1: South Sudan travel advice.

By the time Alex Perry returned to Juba in mid-April 2014, "the violence had been raging for four months. Three state capitals had been razed. Up to 40,000 people were dead. More than a million of South Sudan's population of 6 to 11 million — a measure of the lack of development is that nobody knows for sure — had fled their homes and 250,000 of those had walked abroad. With no one left to tend the farms, the UN was warning that seven million South Sudanese needed food aid and 50,000 children could die of hunger in months. By those figures, the speed and depth of South Sudan's collapse outdid even Syria's."

The evening before Alex Perry was about to head up to Malakal, he asked a government official what the situation was like in that city.

"You will find mostly bones," said the man. "They killed them in the streets and in the churches and in the hospital, then they burned the town to the ground. The dogs and the birds have been at the bones. Malakal isn't there anymore."

It was true, Alex Perry reported. As soon as his plane door opened at the Malakal airport, he could smell the "stench of bloating corpses."

Now, almost exactly one year later, Brock Warner was headed to South Sudan to check out the education projects War Child was funding with local partners in the camps made up of the people who had fled Malakal.

"We were doing projects in Malakal in a camp setting," says Brock, "and we've been doing work in refugee and IDP (Internally Displaced People) camps for years, but we have never been able to document it well, to get really good photos of the work. One year someone came back with photos and there was a thumbprint in the middle of the lens. It was useless. And that's how it came about, the idea for me to go to South Sudan was to document some of our work in the camps there."

Brock began immediate preparations. He had to get security briefings, make arrangements and connect with local South Sudan staff.

Then, a couple of things happened to give the War Child team in Toronto pause.

The first thing was that a British aid worker was shot in South Sudan. There was concern that aid workers might be targeted in the way that Médecins Sans Frontières (MSF) staff had been in Somalia. In 2013 they pulled out of that country after 16 of their people had been killed.

The second consideration was that UNICEF had just reported that 89 boys had been abducted from a school in the Wau Shilluk camp, one of the camps outside Malakal where War Child had a project and where, in fact, Brock was headed.

But it turned out that there was something more to the death of the aid worker. It had been determined it wasn't a targeted killing. And they could keep up on the developments in the UNICEF report with UN people on the ground.

"It came together so fast," Brock said. "In hindsight there were some of these little signs of instability with the aid worker being killed and the abductions. But at the time, I was more concerned with getting my visas and my passport renewed. I did have a second thought when the lady at the passport office lectured me...it was like a motherly lecture...about why I shouldn't be going to South Sudan."

Two other people would make up the War Child team with Brock.

There was Nikki Whaites, the Deputy Director of International Programs at War Child Canada who Brock knew well. Nikki had worked in international aid for more than a decade including four years as international director for Journalists for Human Rights. She had in South Sudan before and had experience working in some of the worlds' difficult regions including Afghanistan, the Democratic Republic of the Congo, Ghana, Iraq, Bangladesh and Haiti, and had been with War Child for four years.

Professional photographer, Jeff Holt, would also be joining them to document their work in the camp. Jeff was an American-living Bangladesh. He had done previous work for War Child.

"I didn't realize it at the time," says Brock now, "but hiring a professional photographer is worth every penny. I don't know how many lens or flashes Jeff was carrying around. I was taking some pictures, but when Jeff turned his MAC book around to show me what he was getting, I just put my camera away."

They were going to meet up in Juba.

Brock left Toronto on a 14-hour flight to Dubai, a nice flight, he says, during which he watched five movies. He spent the night in Dubai and took a regional carrier, Fly Dubai, to Juba.

"It's culture shock right away," says Brock. "I'm flying into Juba in this beautiful plane and it's been a nice flight, but as we get closer I see fire. And I think 'is the airport on fire?' That's what I'm thinking. It wasn't as it turns out, but you could smell the smoke."

The brief Nikki supplied to Brock about what to do and who to speak to when he got to Juba went out the window when they didn't go through the terminal, but got diverted to somewhere else.

"There was this guy sitting under a tree. He's got an infrared thermometer to take our temperature. We had to fill in Ebola forms to certify we didn't have a fever, but I still got picked up by our driver and we headed to the War Child office in Juba which is shared with War Child Netherlands."

The office is inside a nine-foot cement wall with barbed wire on top. It's like a neighbourhood behind the wall.

"People are all over the place," says Brock, "because life happens inside. But it's so odd. It's everything you'd see on the outside, but it's gated."

"We get to the War Child office, which is a great space, meet George Otim, the country director, who is originally from Uganda. He's very calm and collected and the first thing we do is a security briefing."

The next day, after a shower and a rest, Brock and the team head south towards Torit, where they were meeting with a prospective local partner and government officials. They all pile into a Land Cruiser, the Juba team, plus Nikki, Brock and Jeff Holt, the photographer. They drive for four or five hours, past little villages. It's a rural area with lots of opportunity for agriculture. But similar to many countries, food aid has compromised local agricultural production by serving to dry up local agricultural markets and contributing to long-term food insecurity.

But the view didn't look that different from what you'd see on TV. It was beautiful countryside, red dirt roads, grass and mountains that pop up in the distance.

"The further we got from Juba, the worse the roads get. I don't think there's a functioning grid. Everything is on generators," says Brock.

"And the closer we get to Torit, the more skepticism greets us. Like 'who are you,' 'what are you doing here.' We had to make sure Jeff didn't take pictures."

The government of South Sudan doesn't allow photography of any government property and the definition of government property extended beyond government buildings and includes roads, bridges and soldiers (who are everywhere).

"It's really tempting when you see these amazing scenes going by," Brock says. "It's easy to snap a picture, but it might have been the last picture Jeff took with that camera."

Before they visited the project at Nimule, where they would be free to take as many photos as they wanted, the team stopped by local offices in Torit to go through the ritual of speaking to government officials to say how happy they were to be in the area. The next day they drove to Nimule, a town on the border of the Trans African Highway, which crossed between Uganda and South Sudan. The proximity to the highway is why War Child does livelihood projects in Nimule. There's auto repair, mechanics and tailoring courses and, because of the road, and the opportunity for people to come and take them.

They got to the project in time for the graduation ceremony.

"The graduation ceremony lasted all day," Brocks says. "There's a formality to it where everyone gets to make a little speech, often in three languages, English, Arabic and Dinka. But the students' speeches were the best. They would talk about what they learned and how important it was to them. Some of them wrote poems. That was the highpoint. If there was an arc to the trip, that was the highpoint."

There are no commercial flights to Malakal. The UN runs the United Nations Humanitarian Air Service (UNHAS) specifically for UN accredited agencies and UN staff. But other people use the service, like other aid groups or media. You can purchase a ticket. There is a special place on the tarmac for UNHAS planes and passengers get driven out and back from the plane to the terminal.

"Obviously, there's no frills on UNHAS," Brock says. "You get a plastic cup of water and the only reading material is the most recent security briefing they have printed out on paper."

The flight from Juba to Malakal was uneventful and the plane landed safely on the tarmac of Malakal's airport. Brock looked out the window as two pick-up trucks drove out to the plane. There were six UN soldiers in the back of each truck with a mounted gun in the middle. It wasn't what was supposed to happen when they'd been briefed about the circumstances of their arrival.

The plane opened up and the passenger stairs were dropped onto the tarmac. The soldiers stood on either side of the steps forming a line. Brock and the War Child team had to walk straight from the plane into a commuter bus that had just driven up. They drove a short distance and were dropped off at a 20 x 20 foot bunker surrounded by chicken wire. They were escorted inside and the door locked.

"We were confused," said Brock, "because we could still see the airport. But eventually, we get picked up from the bunker to be driven to the UN camp. And we're driving down this long dirt road. But there are big ditches on either side, man-made ditches. In these wide ditches were beds, beds without mattresses, and I find out that the reason for not going through the airport and the reason for the beds lining the road is that rebel groups and the government fight over control of the airport as they fight over control of Malakal and the soldiers sleep there.

"That's why armed guards escorted us from the plane to that secure location. It was, apparently, where we were most vulnerable. And the ditches were also where the bodies would get pushed until they would eventually get picked up."

The team arrived at the camp and went through several sets of guards and checkpoints. A tank was parked outside of a grouping of shipping containers, which made up the humanitarian hub. Another security briefing was given. They were told that if something goes down, they are to go into the shipping container and lock the door until it's safe to come out. They were told they could be in there for days.

"This location is very remote," says Brock, "and Malakal, the camp and the airport are all within a 10 kilometer radius."

The UN camp has a population of about 40,000 people. It's called a "Protection of Civilians" camp or a PoC camp, and is sectioned into PoC 1, PoC 2 or PoC 3 to help give people an "address." These people aren't refugees or classified as internally displaced people although they are displaced because they've been driven from their homes. But everyone in the camp was from Malakal and the surrounding rural areas. And, because of the conflict, they were living a few kilometers from their homes in an armed UN mission camp.

"The humanitarian hub is a small corner in the greater camp. It's where helicopters can land and where we can get food and water," said Brock. "But we're this little postage stamp corner in the rest of the camp. The IOM workers have these shipping containers to run their offices out of."

The IOM is the International Organization for Migration, an organization that was set up in 1950 to help people displaced by World War II and now assists "people who are refugees, displaced or defined as migrants" all over the world.

The shelters where people were living were made from bamboo stakes and tarps or IOM tents. The IOM also distributes non-food items (NFIs).

"The IOM is huge," says Brock, "Once you see their logo, you notice it on everything. They pretty much run the camp. We paid them for staying there. But we didn't get a shipping container. We slept in a tent with about ten people. But there was electricity, an extension cord that was run into the middle of the room."

War Child's local partner is the Upper Nile Youth Development Association or UNDA-Upper Nile. Upper Nile is one of the ten states of South Sudan. Oxfam and War Child had supported the UNDA-Upper Nile offices in Malakal. Prior to the coup, they were raising money locally for a new outdoor lavatory by selling admission to watch soccer games on their office television. Brock went into Malakal with a UNDA Upper Nile's staff person. The razed town was completely deserted except for a small market where a few people were selling fruit, vegetables and some odds and ends.

The UNDA-Upper Nile offices were emptied in December, 2013 when the worst of the bloodshed occurred. The rebels had ransacked it. There was graffiti everywhere.

"You could tell they were young," says Brock, "by what they had written. They had scribbled stuff about J Money on the walls."

Twenty-one-year-old rapper, J Money, was a member of the rap group OTF and was shot and killed in Chicago in September, 2013.

There were still empty shell casings on the ground.

"Originally, our project had been designed for a rural setting. We had to change it around to make it work in a camp setting," said Brock. "The idea of peace building, community building, educational programming and all that stayed the same. It just wasn't happening under a tree."

The local staff had planned a packed itincrary for Brock and the team that included meeting community leaders and students, some of whom were graduating. The younger ones, the young adults wanted to talk about the peace process. There were peace talks happening in Addis Ababa at the time and they were asking questions like "What is Canada doing?" and "What more could Canada be doing?"

"I didn't have great answers for their questions," Brock said. "You can't make promises you can't deliver, so you can't have much of lively debate as I would have liked, however, you can prod and find out what they feel and what they think Canada can be doing."

"They definitely know much more about Canada than Canadians know about South Sudan. It drove home that we need to do a lot of education about the context these programs are happening in. To move back two steps to say…here is south Sudan on a map. Here's how big it is. Here are the languages they speak—trying to tell that story."

"Conventional wisdom in fundraising is to simplify, simplify, simplify; to boil things down to the most striking positioning message that you can and get everything down to a tweet. The more I do this, the less I believe in that idea."

The next day, the team headed to Wau Shilluk, the camp where UNICEF had reported the abduction of 89 boys a couple of weeks before. It was a 30 or 40-minute drive to get to the Nile River where they got on a boat for another 40 minutes.

Brock says "Just like there are Dinkas and Nuers, there are Shilluk people who have been there for longer than anyone has been in Canada. They live on the Nile and make their livelihood off the Nile. They might also have cattle and fishing camps where they move back and forth."

"So this Shilluk settlement, I don't know what it is in its normal size, but it ballooned into almost the same size as the UN camp, 30 or 40 thousand people. But it's not a UN settlement. It's an informal settlement made up of refugees or internally displaced people, who maybe don't feel comfortable in the UN camp. They have their own reasons for wanting to stay in the Wau Shilluk camp but it's not protected with the same order as the UN camp."

"The IOM was doing NFI distribution there. We saw Médecins Sans Frontières (MSF) and I think it might have been the Norwegian Refugee Council (NRC) doing water cleaning and maternal health."

The War Child team needed permission to enter the camp and were stopped at a gated government compound. Brock, Nikki and Jeff were with War Child regional staff, James, Sabit, and Hakim. They would have to show their paperwork.

The abduction of 89 boys from Wau Shilluk had just been reported so there was a lot of attention on the camp. The government was looking closely at it and UNICEF was investigating. The Wau Shilluk authorities were doing their own version of investigation and they weren't happy with the thought of somebody coming in with cameras.

The long wait began.

"While we were waiting, just outside the office, we saw a group of very young soldiers in formation wearing full camouflage uniforms with automatic weapons," says Brock. "They passed by the office door. They looked very young, that I can say for sure. They were in uniform and they had guns. And there were other times we saw very young looking soldiers. The day we went to Malakal and saw the market. There were two young soldiers with AK-47s over their shoulders in full uniform. They were looking at flip flops. In that context, you realize that they're just youngsters, but you don't know how old they were. They didn't look of age. They looked like kids shopping for shoes at the Dufferin Mall."

"It took a while to get it sorted so we could have access to the school. There wasn't much of a conversation. Everything seems to run on the stamps and the signatures, and we had duplicate after duplicate. So whatever we had was obviously indisputable."

They were escorted on the two or three kilometre walk to the education centre and the team had been told not to take their cameras out of their bags. But when Nikki saw War Child flag flying in the air, she took her phone out to take a picture of it. In seconds, four armed soldiers, dressed in camouflage and armed with AK-47s, were within feet of her.

"I don't know where they came from but they wanted to make sure she was not taking a picture of the settlement," says Brock, "which she wasn't, but it showed that there were eyes on us, whether we knew it or not, every single step of the way."

Brock says that when their group got to the War Child project at Wau Skilluk, there was silence.

"It wasn't just the kids," he said. "We talked to teachers, to young adult helpers. They would report on the number of students we've got, they've got a great way of tracking all that. There are ALPs, Accelerated Learning Programs—ALP 1 is like Grade Kindergarten, Grade 1 and 2. ALP 2 is Grades 3, 4 and 5. And that was the discussion. It was open and cordial but there was no the informal stuff like the Malakal PoC camp, about what the camp was like. They didn't want to talk. At all. Because they knew they were being listened to."

"We went to talk to a couple of teachers, but we got very little except what we needed to get. Then we talked to students. They didn't say anything. Their eyes were on the ground. And after not getting anything for 20 minutes, we asked if they had any questions for us? Do you want to know about Canada? And then, they opened up like flowers. 'What kind of trees do you have? What's the weather like? Where is Canada?' And you got the tiny little glimpse of their personalities."

A break in the tension came just as the team was about to leave. The students wanted to do a traditional dance

"They unpacked the shawls and dancing sticks and they got Sabit to join in," said Brock, which he loved. "Even our escorts got into it. One wanted to play the drums. And we realized he was just about 17 or 18. He had been putting on a strong façade, but what he really liked was playing the drums. Everything became normal for about 5 minutes. But when it was done, it all snapped right back to the way it was before."

The group made its way back to the official compound. Just like they had to ask permission to get in, they had to ask for permission to leave. And, once again, they had to wait.

Brock left Wau Shilluk on Friday, was home on Saturday and back in the office on Monday morning with a South Sudan beard and his face peeling from sunburn.

"Did you ever meet Conan MacLean at MSF?" Brock is asking me over coffee. "He's their fundraising manager and he's a bit like me. He's reserved and wants the trains to run on time. He's also MSF's lead Aeroplan contact like I am with War Child. Aeroplan gives us hundreds of thousands of miles every year to fly our people all over the world. They're great. So Conan and I cross paths quite a bit and once a year Aeroplan brings us all together."

"Aeroplan wanted to hear the whole story about the work of War

Child and MSF, not just the good parts," said Brock. "But Conan doesn't like doing presentations so he just read a story off his iPhone so as not to miss a detail."

What he read was a firsthand account from an MSF doctor during the Ebola crisis and he had just had somebody really close to him die from Ebola. This is after seeing so many other people die. His friends and his community were dying all around him. He'd witnessed eight or nine members of one family cut down to a mother and a son. And then the son died.

"Conan choked up as he was reading from his iPhone. He could barely get through it," Brock says. "And to me that was a glimpse at how affected the entire MSF family around the world is feeling about what is going on right now. First they had the Ebola crisis, and now they've had their hospitals bombed in Afghanistan, Syria and Yemen."

"I think MSF have lost patience with trying to tell a story that's not as close to the truth as possible," says Brock. "I feel like I've lost my patience a bit too. Ten years of fundraising starts to indoctrinate you, encourage you to be strategic, to professionalize the sector, to invest in governance and accountability. There's a place for all of this within the organization, but for a front-line person...the challenges I have in reflecting on this is less what the experience of the conflict and the fighting meant to me. That story belongs to the people in the camps and the local partners who are working with them. I wish all my donors could have such a personal connection to the work in the field. It's impossible, I know. We're not going to get them all out to South Sudan. But I'm trying to figure out what the next best thing is."

———

Epilogue: Not long after Brock left Wau Shilluk, authorities restricted access to aid agencies. Schools were closed and teachers fled. On March 12 2015, the government announced that the 89 school children abducted in Wau Shilluk by forces loyal to Johnson Olony were released. The Committee for the Eradication of Abduction of Women and Children says they had been negotiating with Johnson Olony to release the children. The move came after the UN intensified calls for the release of the children. By the fall of 2015, through a process of negotiation between the authorities and aid organizations, access by air and water were re-established.

On February 17 and 18 2016, a new wave of violence broke out in Malakal with MSF reporting 150 people injured. Then, on February 18, fighting broke out in the Malakal Protection of Civilian (PoC) site killing 18, including two MSF South Sudanese staff members. MSF reported, "during the fighting, armed actors engaged in widespread and intentional destruction of humanitarian services and the shelters of displaced persons in the PoC."

8 /

Solving the World's
Most Wicked Problems

It's coming up onto almost a decade of bad mojo for the international development sector.

In her 2009 book, *Dead Aid*, Dambisa Moyo called development aid to African nations a "malignant" force and marked a cascade of critique, scandal and revelation that the sector seems unable or unwilling to counter.

Moyo's books popularized the idea that aid from "donor" countries, child sponsorship and rock musicians is actually contributing to the intransigent poverty and conflict on that continent; turning the Bob Geldof and Bono inspired *Live Aid* movement on its head.

Of course, Dambisa Moyo was not the first person to ever publish a critique of foreign aid. Peter Bauer, who was born in Budapest in 1915 and died in 2002 in London at the age of 87, taught at the London School of Economics and was considered one of the greatest development economists in history. Bauer was a committed libertarian who spent his entire career opposing state-sponsored foreign aid and defined it as "a transfer of resources from the *taxpayer* of one donor country to the *government* of a recipient country." He was a contemporary of Milton Friedman, the Nobel-winning, free-market adherent who advised President Ronald Reagan and Prime Minister Margaret Thatcher, and who, along with John Maynard Keynes, his philosophical opposite, was considered the most influential economist of the 20th century.

Both Bauer and Friedman extolled the values of the free market system and limited government, and Bauer felt a market approach would be better for poorer countries in Africa. Individuals would be better off, he said, since so little of the aid the state received made it to the individual and that anyone actually looking at the data would have to draw the same conclusion.

William Easterly, the current co-director of New York

University's Development Research Institute and also influenced by Friedman, published *The White Man's Burden: Why the West's Efforts to Aid the Rest Have Done So Much Ill and So Little Good* in 2006, three years before Moyo's book. Moyo essentially said the same thing as Bauer adding that state-sponsored aid encouraged authoritarianism. A review of Easterly's book written by Virgina Postrel and published in the *New York Times Sunday Book Review* said, "Easterly asks the right questions, combining compassion with clear-eyed empiricism. Bono and his devotees should heed what he has to say."

So what Dambisa Moyo was saying wasn't exactly new, but her perspective decidedly was. Her book took the *New York Times* Best Seller List by storm.

In his foreword for *Dead Aid*, British historian, Niall Ferguson, who had just published his own 2008 bestseller, *The Ascent of Money,* said, "the simple fact that *Dead Aid* is the work of an African black woman is the least of the reasons why you should read it. But it's a reason nonetheless."

The Zambian-born and raised, and Harvard and Oxford educated, economist was an in-demand guest on the talk show circuit. In the world of television, it didn't hurt that Moyo was confidant, articulate and a sharp dresser. As Niall Ferguson pointed out, she was a voice in need of amplification, the experience of developmental aid from an African woman's perspective.

"Fundamentally," said Dambisa Moyo, "I think Africa doesn't need more aid. It needs governments to be made accountable to the domestic citizenry and not to donors. Africans stand in the hot African sun to elect their leaders, and it's those leaders who are charged with the responsibility of delivering social services and being accountable to people."

"Because, in reality, Africans should be making a choice between the Canadian International Development Agency (CIDA) and the United Nations Development Agency (UNDA) because that's where the money is coming from."

The response to Moyo's book was scathing and the perceived proximity of her views to economists like Milton Friedman made her immediately suspect to some.

Pulitzer-prize winning author and *New York Times* writer, Nicholas Kristof, wrote that "Moyo attracted attention in part because of the novelty of an African denouncing aid to Africa" and that her book set off another wave of feuding between two camps of humanitarians.

Madelaine Bunting, a U.K. writer with the *Guardian* newspaper, and author of *Willing Slaves: How the Overwork Culture is Ruling Our Lives* said, "The danger is that this book will get more attention than it deserves."

Bunting argued the book was dangerous, irrelevant and that Moyo was a shill for protectionists.

"The problem is that this kind of analysis (much of which is now only of historical relevance) provides ammunition for those who are skeptical of international responsibilities and always keen to keep charity at home. Here they have the perfect protagonist to advance their arguments: an African woman who speaks their language."

She regarded Moyo's bona fides with suspicion and called her motives into question.

"The author, Dambisa Moyo, worked for Goldman Sachs (a fact about which the dust jacket is strangely coy) after a period of time at the World Bank and a doctorate at Oxford. One suspects that behind this book is a remarkable woman with an impressive career and very little time for learning how to write a good book...Despite being poorly argued, *Dead Aid* will boost Moyo's profile."

"Few people fight as savagely as humanitarians," Nicholas Kristof wrote. But, he argued that the examples Moyo had cited were out-of-date and the aid model had become more modern, pragmatic and creative…and that aid organizations were now doing more "empirical" work on the success of their projects.

"I don't mean to imply that building brick and mortar schools is an outmoded idea," he added. "My wife and I built a school in Cambodia…because we were able to establish teachers do show up there. All sides…have merit."

Moyo shot back at her critics saying in an interview with the Australia Broadcasting Corporation (ABC) that there are too many people who have a vested interest in the continual cycle of Africa in despair to justify their existence.

"I'm talking about academics," she says. "I'm talking about the NGO community. I'm talking about policy makers and politicians who know this doesn't work. The evidence shows it doesn't work. In 1970, 10 per cent of Africans lived in poverty. Now, more like 70 per cent, in many countries as high as 80 per cent of Africans are living in poverty."

She argued that government-to-government aid fuels corruption, induces unrest because aid is pooling at the top, creates a debt burden, kills exports and disenfranchises citizens because African governments spend their time courting donors, as opposed to taxpayers, so they're not interested in what their people have to say.

"An aid model makes good leaders bad and bad leaders worse. It's free money. There are no strings attached," she says, and that discarding the aid model will affect the African elite as opposed to the broader population because that's where the money is going now.

She says that in 60 years, $1 trillion in aid has been transferred to Africa with no increase in growth or decrease in poverty levels.

She argues for African countries to use capital markets as a way for countries to start to fund themselves. In the book, she prescribes a five-year plan where aid from donor countries is reduced and where government focuses on:

- Getting credit ratings for their country.
- Learning how to pitch to potential investors.
- Raising money from the markets.
- Raising capital from China and the Middle East.

The view of Moyo as capitalist interloper was widespread.

Stephen Lewis, former United Nations Ambassador for Canada and United Nations' special envoy for HIV/AIDS, and the founder of the eponymous Stephen Lewis Foundation, feels strongly about the aid agenda. He took part in a Munk Debate in 2009 where he was partnered with Paul Collier, professor of economics and public at the University of Oxford.

The question was, "Be it resolved, foreign aid does more harm than good."

Moyo's debating partner was Peruvian economist, Hernando De Soto. DeSoto is a leading thinker on property rights in poor countries and wrote *The Mystery of Capital: Why Capitalism Triumphs in the West and Fails Everywhere Else.*

In a nod to the most virulent critics of the book, Lewis, in his opening debate statement said, although he is a critic of Moyo's book, he had "none of the jugular instinct that some of her detractors have displayed." But what Dambisa Moyo's book fails to acknowledge, he says, "is the huge impact aid has had on the humanitarian imperative."

"Millions of people with AIDS are alive today who without anti-retroviral drugs would be dead. Millions of children have been immunized against fatal diseases. Over 30 million international children are in school since the year 2000; modest reductions in extreme poverty from 58 per cent to 51 per cent in 1999 and 2007; malaria death rates cut in half in countries like Rwanda and Ethiopia in the course of two years because of insecticide-treated bed nets. I could go on ad infinitum. This is aid. Aid that gets to the grassroots. Aid that transforms hope in communities. It is no small matter. It is no band-aid."

"To be honest, I think the whole aid model is built on pity," responded Dambisa Moyo. "It emanates from a pity for Africa. Africa cannot do it. It cannot achieve growth and sadly because there are no incentives for African governments not to take aid, we've basically ended up in a situation where it doesn't work and people are just happy to keep it going."

Moyo says that issues with the credit crisis and ensuing recession have made people within the NGO sector, who live in capitalist societies themselves, even more critical of the capitalist system. But that sixty years of an aid-dependent model which has increased poverty, sown conflict and made leaders unaccountable to their people has only increased calls for more aid.

"That, to me," she says, "is intellectual dishonesty, particularly from the quarters of people who are big proponents of capitalism in other parts of the world. But when it comes to Africa, they are big supporters of aid."

Robert Fox was the Executive Director of Oxfam Canada for 10 years, from 2005 to 2014. He has a long history in the international development sector having also worked in Central America for Oxfam. He remembers when *Dead Aid* was published.

"There was an intense dynamic around that book," he says. "And I agreed with the analysis. It trumpeted foreign investment, which Oxfam had advocated in every report for 10 years prior to that. If you have a rights-based approach, as Oxfam does, you believe that govern-ment has to have a responsibility to provide a safe and healthy society." But, he felt Moyo's prescription was not realistic and that she focused on the worst of the sector, without acknowledging the good work. On the other hand, he says, "the response from the sector was too defensive."

———

While the iNGO sector generally did not demonstrate much open-ness to the idea of promoting capitalism in Africa, in other parts of the world, some iNGOs were hard at work building partnerships with capitalists of the most committed kind.

Canada is the world's largest player in mining. Seventy-five per cent of the world's mining companies are based in Canada.

World Vision, one of the world's largest aid organizations that, in 2015, generated $442 million in Canada and $2.27 billion USD worldwide, was one of the first of many iNGOs to hook up with the mining sector.

In 2007, a partnership with Barrick Gold was facilitated through the Canadian International Development Agency's (CIDA's) as part of the emerging Corporate Social Responsibility (CSR) Strategy.

Barrick Gold made an investment of $1.3 million on a proj-ect in Laguna Notre, Peru to develop nutrition, education, and employment skills projects and support World Vision's mandate to "empower the poor to build a better future for themselves and their children through sustainable development."

The World Vision project was one among many. The *Globe and Mail* reported that, according to CIDA's project database, CIDA has approved "at least $50 million CAD in projects that are linked to the mining industry in countries such as Peru and Burkina Faso since the Conservatives came to power in 2006."

But the Laguna Notre project wasn't the only time Barrick Gold and World Vision have come together in the past decade. In 2012, the charity partnered with Barrick Gold on the development of a mine in Quirulvilca and another in one Pierina. There were investments of roughly $1 million CAD at each site. In the promotion of the partnership, Barrick Gold touted its successes in the region:

- 4,000 jobs for Peruvian workers in the region during construction of mines.
- 1,500 employed working with Barrick after construction.
- Safest and most environmentally responsible miners in the region.
- "Proven" commitment to address environmental, educational, and health issues...a model corporate engagement.

World Vision Canada defended the partnership as having a positive impact on children and families.

"We have to be realistic here, there is self-interest on the part of every party," said World Vision Canada then-president Dave Toycen. "Anything we can do to encourage and advocate for better mining practices, and support the communities that they are displacing or affecting, we're contributing to a better lifestyle and environment for them."

But there were problems in the mining areas. Damage to the region's water source caused by mining activities became a main source of conflict between Barrick Gold and local communities. At the World Vision/Barrick Gold partnership sites, protests by residents and indigenous populations were happening regularly, contributing to the roughly 200-300 conflicts between mining companies and the population that occur in Peru every year.

Miguel Palacin Quispe, General Coordinator of CAOI (Andean Coordinating Committee of Indigenous Organizations), wrote a letter to CIDA, via the Minister of International Cooperation, Bev Oda, asking the Canadian government not to pursue the CSR Strategy of teaming up mining companies and charities like World Vision.

He wrote that mining by Canadian companies created conflicts in the region because of dispossession of lands, destruction of water sources, and ignoring of internationally recognized rights (ILO Convention 169, the UN Declaration of Rights of Indigenous Peoples). Despite the goals of CSR, "no 'social work' carried out with the mining companies can compensate for the damage done…"

In 2012, the National Tribunal on Water Justice in Peru found Barrick Gold to be the second top company damaging water sources at five lakes near Laguna Sur (close to the Laguna Norte site) and cited severe pollution impacting crops and small-scale livestock farming.

Opinion among charity observers on international charities forming partnerships with mining companies is mixed.

Fundraising veteran, Ken Wyman says, "Generally speaking, corporations are moving into the CSR (Corporate Social Responsibility) sector in a much more dramatic way. Soap is probably the most obvious example, but there are all kinds of examples where Coke sets up feel-good projects and Tampax sends products to Africa. It's self-serving, yes, because they are going to want you to use the products afterwards."

Wyman says at one level he's a little uncomfortable defending the mining sector, but that companies have always given where their employees are. If a mining company is based in Sudbury, for example, then they are going to make a donation to the local hospital. People may be annoyed that the mining company has created some of the problems that the hospital is clearing up, but they are a major employer in the community and they should contribute.

"Why should that be any different if it's a remote community... where the mining company is the biggest employer. It is creating some of the problems, so they should be the biggest contributor in community campaigns. At its best, it's a very benign form of the evolution of capitalism. It's moved along from 'we mess it up and we leave' to 'we mess it up and we try to fix it up.' Would it be better if they didn't mess it up in the first place? Sure, but that's not happening...because we all buy cell phones that require rare minerals that are only found in remote communities."

Robert Fox, formerly of Oxfam Canada, says a number of mining companies were very interested in working with them. We declined, he said.

"They actually called Oxfam GB (Great Britain) up to see if Oxfam Canada could be overruled. They thought we were under their supervision. But it doesn't work that way." Oxfam affiliates are separately incorporated. But there was no doubting the influence of the Canadian mining industry says Fox. "We were told by our partners in Central America that the Canadian Ambassador was referred to as the 'Minister of Mines.'"

Fox sees iNGOs partnering with mining companies as naïve and opportunistic, and in some instances as unhelpful and inappropriate.

"There are degrees," he says. "You might have an established program already in a community and provide a forum for consultation with that community, then maybe it's appropriate. But these were new projects based on commercial interests in the community. Parachuting in, even with the intention of doing good work...I'm

147

skeptical about how you can do that with integrity."

"Some NGOs found themselves in the spotlight in a way they didn't expect. They were getting heat from their own donors. Some would acknowledge that it was an error."

———

Apart from the deep division on the efficacy of international aid in the past decade, the sector was rocked by one of the biggest fundraising scandals in its history, the type of scandal everyone can understand, a scandal about fundraising and money.

It centered on one of the poorest countries in the world where the annual per capita income is USD $350, life expectancy is 62.7 years and there are 25 doctors for every 100,000 people. The Gross Domestic Product is USD $8.5 billion.

The 2010 earthquake in Haiti, population 10 million, occurred just before suppertime on January 12th. The ground shook with a tremor that measured 7.0 on the Richter scale, a catastrophic level, with the epicenter 25 kilometres west of the capital, Port au Prince. It was a humanitarian disaster. More than 200,000 people were killed. Tens of thousands of more were pulled out of the rubble.

The city of Port au Prince and the surrounding area were devastated. Three and a half million people were affected.

Many countries responded to the call for humanitarian aid. So much so, there was a traffic jam of international charities swirling around the small country, which shares the island of Hispaniola with Dominican Republic. Hundreds of millions of dollars were raised for the emergency relief and re-building effort.

The American Red Cross alone collected USD $500 million

from its own fundraising efforts and through unsolicited gifts from concerned Americans.

Four and a half years later, the American Red Cross was awash in scandal. National Public Radio (NPR) and ProPublica, a news outlet that describes itself as a nonprofit newsroom that produces investigative journalism in the public interest, reported, "It was difficult to know where all the money went."

Reporters spoke to Jean-Max Bellerive and Joel Boutroue, the Haiti prime minister and UN special representative in Haiti at the time of the quake. They considered Red Cross's claim that all the money went to helping four and a half million Haitians get back on their feet to be questionable.

Bellerive said is it just wasn't possible, that four and a half million people were not in the area affected by the earthquake. Boutroue said that number would encompass all the urban areas in Haiti in 2010.

The issue was more than one of poetic exaggeration.

NPR and ProPublica reported "the Red Cross says that it has provided homes to more than 130,000 people, but the number of permanent homes the charity has built is six." Also it was reported that internal issues delayed services, that the Red Cross never had a plan for Haiti, and responded slowly to fight the cholera outbreak that followed ten months after the earthquake.

The American Red Cross firmly and completely denied all the charges in the NPR/ProPublica reports saying, "4.5 million had been affected by the disease prevention program" and that they'd "leveraged the skillsets of 47 partners."

Robert Fox says the problems with the American Red Cross arose because core competency of the Red Cross is their emergency preparedness, resources and relief. "In the context of development work, emergency relief is a relatively inexpensive competency. It is complex, but not expensive and takes place in days, weeks and months."

But because the American Red Cross collected so much money—more money than could be spent on emergency efforts—they switched over to doing development work in Haiti, which is not their area of expertise and is a much longer and much more expensive slog.

"With the American Red Cross, a lot of the money they raised didn't go to Haiti and the money that did go was high cost aid," he says.

NPR and ProPublica reported the Red Cross kept soliciting money well after it had enough for the emergency relief that is the group's stock in trade.

"That story was painful for me to hear," says Fox.

A few international aid organizations were already taking a different approach. In a move that stunned charity observers, after the 2004 tsunami Médecins Sans Frontières decided to stop fundraising for tsunami response.

"When MSF got as much money as it could spend in tsunami emergency efforts, they put that message up on their website offering people the opportunity to donate to other work," Robert Fox says. "It was brilliantly appropriate and I wish more organizations would do it. We do have the capacity to signal that to the public and it was a brilliant moment for the sector. Real leadership."

MSF took a similar approach with fundraising for the Haitian earthquake. In its report on the disaster, they stated,

Following the earthquake, MSF initially developed fundraising activities and the generosity of people around the world in

response to the tragedy that befell Haiti has been overwhelming. While the MSF medical relief effort was immediately shaping up to be massive in volume, the total of funds donated to MSF by the public specifically for this emergency threatened to eclipse what MSF could foresee to spend.

While MSF continued to welcome donations, pro-active earmarked fundraising for Haiti was put on hold. Instead, MSF called upon donors to continue to support the organization for its current and future emergency work in general.

As of 31 May, four-and-a-half months after the earthquake, MSF had received around 91 million euros earmarked for emergency relief in Haiti, and had already spent nearly 53 million euros on assistance to the Haitian population. MSF foresees to spend around 89 million euros in Haiti until the end of the year.

—•—

While reports of the story behind the devastating southern Somalia famine in 2011 received less attention than the American Red Cross scandal, it also shook some sector observers to their core.

Perhaps the most startling has been the revelation that the famine had less to do with the drought in the region and more to do with keeping three million people starving in order to make sure three or four thousand *al-Shabaab* terrorists didn't accidently get fed.

The strategy was, journalist Alex Perry reported, a result of the U.S. anti-terror campaign that banned most aid groups from helping.

Alex Perry explained on CBC's *The Current* in January 2016 that people knew a year before it happened that the famine was coming. There's a system in drought prone East Africa called the Early Famine Warning that had been sounded a year before. Food aid had been shipped and stored in preparation for the disaster that everybody knew was on the way. It was stocked up in northern Kenya, Uganda, Ethiopia, Djibouti. Everywhere *except* southern Somalia.

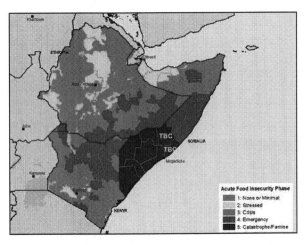

Figure 8.1: July 19 Map by the FEWS-NET (The Famine Early Warning Systems Network)

It took Alex Perry very little investigation to find out the reasons for this food aid gap in southern Somalia he says.

He told radio host Anna Maria Tremonti that the Somali Prime Minister, the Somali Defense Minister, the Minister for Presidential Affairs told him that this was, essentially, strategy. "It was deliberate. They were withholding aid as part of a military strategy to put pressure on *al-Shabaab* to prevent food aid from going into some areas under the control of terrorist organizations."

The plan worked all too well. To put pressure on three or four thousand people belonging to *al-Shabaab*, over 3 million were plunged into famine. The result was more than 250,000 men, women and children died of starvation.

Alex Perry called the events "a war crime that ranked only behind the genocides in Cambodia and Rwanda."

"I've never seen dying like this," Perry said about visiting the children's ward of the only functioning hospital in Mogadishu with Swiss photographer, Dominic Nahr. The ward was a small room containing seven or eight beds.

"Dominic was taking pictures and I was talking to some of the mothers of some of the kids that were lying in the beds," Perry remembers. "I'm pretty sure I was talking to one mother when her boy died…you hate to bring yourself and your own feelings into this amount of suffering…it's still hard to deal with. I couldn't shake the idea that I was in this small room with these kids that were dying and that the room must be filled with their last breaths—so therefore Dominic and I must be breathing in their last breath. I just couldn't shake [it] you know? To this day I still think about that a lot."

"I was in South Sudan, Ethiopia and Kenya at the same time as the famine," says Robert Fox. "There is no question that there is interplay, no question that some aid agencies are service agencies for their government. They see themselves as Blackwater on the nonprofit side."

"I'm not trying to be holier that thou here, but you have to respect international humanitarian law and NGOs who allow themselves to be instruments of their governments' policies put their staff at risk," he adds.

"The simple reality is that to operate in the most at-risk environments where people are facing the greatest need, unfortunately, you do have to sometimes gain permission from some of the belligerents to the conflict," said Samantha Nutt, a doctor with 16 years of experience working in war zones in response to Alex Perry. She is the Executive Director of War Child Canada.

"You have to negotiate for the safety and security of your staff. And this isn't just true in Somalia. It's true in Syria. It's true in Iraq. It's true in South Sudan. All around the world. And it is the case that sometimes aid gets misappropriated and you have to be able to monitor and evaluate and so you do need that safe passage. Unfortunately, we always try to maximize our good intentions, each and every single one of us, but there aren't any guarantees and we're operating in a humanitarian environment that becomes more and more complicated every day."

"With regards to Somalia, the job was to get food to people who need it," said Robert Fox. "Who they are doesn't matter. But international aid groups were timid and the populations who didn't receive the 'Good Housekeeping Seal of Approval,' didn't get [aid]. There is cooptation of the NGO sector. It is a sector that is often naïve about the causes and the symptoms of the causes."

"At the end of the day, we need to address causes in a systematic way."

Meanwhile in Somalia, Perry says international NGOs from Europe, Canada and the U.S were having fundraising campaigns, whose basic line was "there's another famine in Africa. It's horrendous, send us money and we will help fix it."

"It's a narrative about African helplessness and Western generosity, right?" says Perry, "and it's almost completely wrong. This was a famine deliberately caused."

Samantha Nutt says she agrees with Perry "in the context that there's something very wrong with our idea of charity and the way that we approach it; we often don't recognize our own complicity and our own hypocrisies in that equation."

Perry says, "the aid organizations resisted but when the U.S. reminded all of them that it was their biggest donor, they fell into line."

"Constraints are placed on NGOs when they are seen as helping 'enemies of the state,'"says Robert Fox.

"But today, the world is filled with governments who were enemies of the state at one time. Anyone who has anything to do with Hamas, for example, is seen as consorting with terrorists. But Hamas is the government that rules the Gaza Strip."

Fox says that Western governments can put their own interests ahead of people who need aid in other, seemingly more benign, ways but it's there all the same.

"In Afghanistan, the Canadian government wanted to put a friendly face on its involvement. So it gave out knapsacks for children to use when they went to school and the knapsacks had little maple leafs on them which, of course, made these students targets."

Perry wrote extensively about the famine in Somalia including a ten-page piece in *Time* magazine, a magazine he calls "the biggest circulation English language news magazine on the planet." He says that because of the nature of the charges he was leveling and the impact of where the story was published, he expected "a firestorm from the State Department, who were primarily responsible for this policy [and] from all the aid agencies."

But he said there was nothing. No outcry.

"What's unusual about Somalia is it's not often that you find an instance where the West is using food as a weapon," Perry says. That asks some very fundamental questions about the independence of aid and about, really, whether NGOs today have moved so far from their original founding points, which was as *non-governmental* organizations. Are they essentially the implementers of Western foreign policy?

"In the end, the U.S. realized what was going on, rescinded its aid ban and told the aid groups that they could resume food aid deliveries to Somalia," says Perry. "But by the end of July 2011 when the famine was at its height, it was just too late."

In 2013 Morten Jerven wrote a book.

Dr. Jerven is an economic historian with a particular interest in economic development statistics.

He was awarded a PhD from the London School of Economics and since 2009 has been working at the School for International Studies at Simon Fraser University in Vancouver, Canada. In 2014 he was appointed as Associate Professor in Global Change and International Relations at Noragrica at the Norwegian University of Life Sciences. His work is considered "innovative in investigating the construction of African growth data and showing how data quality issues are critical for the evaluation of economic performance."

His book was awarded the 2013 Foreign Affairs Magazine Best Book of the Year. It was titled *Poor Numbers: How We Are Misled by African Development Statistics and What to Do about It*, and it was considered a landmark publication because it pointed out that "the paucity of accurate statistics is not merely a technical problem; it has a massive impact on the welfare of citizens in developing countries."

Jerven says, "One of the most urgent challenges in African economic development is to devise a strategy for improving statistical capacity. The current catchphrase in the development community is 'evidence-based policy,' and scholars are applying increasingly sophisticated econometric methods—but no statistical techniques can substitute for partial and unreliable data."

Michael Hobbes who has worked in the international development sector and who writes in *The New Republic* says he's been involved in projects where their success was "measured on the number of Facebook likes we got, how many pages our summary reports were, how many trips to the field we made."

He writes that Madagascar hasn't had a census since 1993 and the Nigerian census in 2006 was "mired in controversy, politicians accused of inflating numbers to increase political, ethnic and religious representation for their districts."

He cites Amanda Glassman, a member of the Data for Africa Working Group who says, "most of the development statistics—how many people can read, who is at risk of starvation—come from household surveys, many of which are carried out by international monitoring and evaluation teams checking to see whether NGOs are spending donor money wisely."

The problem with these surveys is that they're not aligned between donors, Hobbes says, so, for example, the Bill and Melinda Gates Foundation team comes to a village, asks everybody their age and their weight and what they've been vaccinated for. Next month, other group comes by to ask their height and their education level and how well they can read. Meanwhile, he says, these surveys are not shared between donors and with the local statistics office mandated to gather this kind of information.

Nobel-prize winning economist, Angus Deaton, honoured for his analysis of consumption, poverty, and welfare in 2015 also has significant concerns about measurement.

"There are many tools out there for people who want to make

the world a better place," he said in his Nobel acceptance speech at the University of Stockholm. "The key here is measurement as honest score-keeping to find out whether something is working or whether it's not working at all. In a world where you work entirely in averages, things like inequality and poverty are simply not legible without the detail of individuals." He further says that measurement and data collection is particularly weak when it comes to work being done in Africa.

"Replacement of local authorities by international NGOs might even be partly responsible for Liberia and Sierra Leone's slow response to the Ebola outbreaks," says medical anthropologist, James Pfeiffer.

"After decades of being bypassed by international health charities, local public health services didn't know about, and weren't able to respond to, conditions in their own country. When international foundations come in with their own statistical programs and skip the local authorities, the locals are cut out of information about their own country."

Morten Jerven sums the matter up by saying that no matter how sophisticated your data analysis is, if your raw data is not representative, it's not useful information.

"You can't make bold extrapolations from meager data points."

⸺

The past decade in international development is forcing—or should be forcing—a re-think of the assumptions that have held the sector together for 60 years. The questions are large and unsettling, weighing heavily, like storm clouds, over international aid charities and over the poorest people in the world who, in so many ways, are at their mercy. Is it time for Western activists to demand that Africans have more direct involvement in setting their own development path? To come to grips with some of the results of state-sponsored aid?

Are mining company partnerships with iNGOs pragmatic and obvious or opportunistic and naïve with calamitous consequences for the developing countries involved?

Is aligning themselves too closely with governments putting international aid staff at risk and potentially causing great harm to people in war-ravaged, crisis-ridden countries?

Is any of data used to evaluate aid programs in Africa even remotely adequate for consideration of the best interest of the people involved?

The questions go unanswered. The impetus for change remains elusive because there's an even bigger pre-occupation in the iNGO sector that dwarfs all other discussions. It's a discussion that top-level leadership is increasingly distracted by. It's about a threat to the sector's very survival.

9 /

The Wolf at the Door

Every year, international NGOs have to put more resources into raising the same amount of money they raised in the previous year.

The competition is fierce. Fundraising revenue is flat-lining. Scandal and frustration have had their impact.

But then so has the lack of understanding most donors have about the high cost of operating in complex locations and, of course, the not entirely erroneous notion of large iNGOs as having become unresponsive bureaucracies that are out of touch with the consequences of their actions. People are worn down.

Couple that with the new generations of donors who are not content to give out of a sense of duty, but need to see "with their own eyes" the impact of their beneficence and you have a large, amorphous sector expanding and contracting in places it never knew it had.

The totality of the environment has given rise to do-it-yourself (DIY) charity where people by-pass the traditional iNGOs and manage their own contact with people or projects in the developing world.

"People feel like they can do better themselves and start their own organizations," says Robert Fox. And they will invest their time and money, and the money and time of their networks, in activities that are a result of the needs they, themselves, perceive as urgent to be met.

Larger groups of people every year are doing something similar to what *New York Times* reporter, Nicholas Kristof, and his wife did—build a school in Cambodia.

"It's the Uber-ization of fundraising," says Ken Wyman. "Crowd-funding campaigns for an individual that's in a car accident, a family with a sick child or to help the people of Syria are the new normal. It's another piece of the charitable sector getting worn away by people who say, 'a bunch of neighbours can do this, we don't need another charity in the world,'" says Ken.

Options are also available for the less ambitious donor.

Alternatives like givedirectly.org allow you to connect with a poor person half a world away (conveniently vetted by givedirectly.org) and with a few clicks of a mouse, your money will be deposited in the bank account of a poor person within hours.

Givedirectly.org is the brainchild of "a small venture-backed, NY-based team," supported by Facebook cofounder, Dustin Moskovitz and is "using technology to help the world's poorest."

Givedirectly.org positions itself in direct opposition to traditional iNGOs.

"Traditional ways of giving internationally are complex," they say.

"Donors typically give to international NGOs that manage money, fundraise, and implement programs through partner organizations abroad, which have their own (usually hidden) cost structures. Overall it is hard for donors to tell how their money will be used, what this will cost, and whether there is any evidence that it works."

Givedirectly.org has a solution.

"We have created a simpler way: we take money from donors and give it to the poor" they say, and "we can do this because modern payments technology has drastically cut the costs of sending money directly to the extreme poor at the same time as new research has shown the powerful effects this has on their lives."

Givedirectly.org has a three-step technology-driven process to pick recipients. As outlined on their website:

1. Using publicly available data, we locate extremely poor communities and send field staff door-to-door to digitally collect data on poverty and enroll recipients.

2. We use physical checks, image verification, GPS coordinates, crowd sourced labor and data consistency checks to make sure the recipients are eligible. We have experimented with using satellite imagery.

3. We electronically transfer recipient households roughly $1,000, or around one year's budget for a typical household.

Givedirectly.org is not without confidence and views "direct giving [as] the benchmark against which the old, top-down models are evaluated."

Operations like DIY charities and givedirectly.org are indications we have come full circle to a charitable response that focuses on poor individuals as opposed to more complex systemic problems.

They are very much modern-day twists on child sponsorship where "deserving" adults are substituted for a child. The symbolism, which infantilizes entire populations could not be more striking. It is a budding industry where donations to charity is based on the need to see a grateful (and deserving) individual, cap in hand, at the other end of the line. Potentially, if we follow the techniques of givedirectly.org, an electronic ankle bracelet could be rationalized as part of the mix.

The focus on fundraising for individuals, which organizations like World Vision still employs has been the stock in trade of much international aid work. Plan International (formerly Foster Parents Plan) changed its name in 2006 to "better reflect how we work."

The individualistic approach, they knew, wasn't helping with a more sophisticated understanding of what the issues really were.

Even World Vision will tell you that when you sponsor a child, it is the community of the child you sponsor that receives help, not specifically only that one child.

But the desire for that person-to-person connection runs deep, especially in international development aid where, through decades of marketing child sponsorship, that idea has been deeply carved into the Western charitable psyche.

———

A missionary named Bob Pierce started World Vision in 1950. In 1947, he had joined an evangelical organization called Youth for Christ, after he'd returned from Africa deeply concerned about the poverty and disease he'd witnessed there.

As legend has it, he talked to a fellow member in Youth for Christ, an up-and-coming ad executive named Russ Reid and together they pioneered the widespread use of child sponsorship as a fundraising tool. Russ Reid developed and implemented a marketing plan for the World Vision organization that included direct mail and, later on, television to tell the World Vision story.

The international development sector has used direct marketing extensively ever since.

Child sponsorship was suited to direct mail. It was an emotional and straightforward appeal that cut through a hornet's nest of complexity about why African nations were poor. It made a plea on behalf of the innocent—one child.

It incorporated automatic monthly giving into the structure. For six decades World Vision and organizations like it—Foster Parents Plan, Christian Children's Fund—attracted and kept donors by setting up comprehensive child sponsorship programs where donors agree to make a donation of $20, $30 or $40 a month to support a child. Some families supported two or three children. It was tremendously cost effective and although the aid never quite worked in that kind of personal way, donors felt connected to the children. Fridges throughout the Western world were adorned with their pictures.

In the past decade and a half, the dynamics of direct marketing have changed. It's become much harder to acquire and retain donors.

What started as a spacious market was flooded with mailings from charities of all descriptions requesting help and changes were afoot in the demographic of people who responded to direct mail.

Sending cheques to charities is a channel largely used by older people, older women in particular, who were raised during the depression and felt a duty to give something to those "less fortunate." They didn't expected recognition. The gift was made from a sense of duty. Also, direct mail responsive donors were enthusiastic in their giving, often donating to up to twenty charities using the mail.

But by the 2000s this female elderly demographic was dying off, and the baby boomers following in their wake were not temperamentally suited to altruism or giving money with no recognition. The result was a big shake up in any organization relying on direct marketing, which included almost all international NGOs.

The past decade or two has been hugely challenging says Robert Fox. "The market and demographics were changing," he says. "With direct mail, there was a feeling of 'the last one out, turn off the lights.' We needed new strategies and new channels."

Those new channels included the development of the Direct Response Television (DRTV), pioneered by Russ Reid, where hourlong TV programs were made with celebrity hosts and dramatic footage from the field edited together with regular asks, usually for a monthly donation occurring every 10 minutes or so.

The programs were paid for and produced by the charity and time was purchased on cable channels. Results were studied and the best DRTV-responsive slots on the daily schedule were soon determined, as were likely gift amounts, and at what moment a gift was made during the broadcast. With this empirical data, DRTV, just like the direct mail campaigns that preceded it, was honed into a science including the knowledge that by following a certain format and attaining average results, a DRTV campaign would take about 18 to 21 months to pay for itself.

But after a decade of boom time, the DRTV market became saturated. Big charities bought all the best time slots and everyone else was left to scrabble over what remained.

"Unless you have the economies of scale, DRTV doesn't really work," says Robert Fox. Oxfam Canada was one of those charities that didn't have those economies and Oxfam has never used child sponsorship as a fundraising tool, which would make a channel like DRTV harder to succeed in.

In the hope of attracting a younger demographic, many international aid groups got into the face-to-face (F2F) business.

F2F is street solicitation by teams of passionate and informed young people dressed in smart aprons identifying them as part of the charity and carrying clipboards in their hands. The technique, developed by Greenpeace in Europe, was so successful that many others, especially iNGOs, tried it for themselves.

Face-to-face fundraising is, however, labour intensive (expensive) and required training large groups of transient workers. Similar to direct mail and DRTV, consultancies sprang up that specialized in F2F; businesses that charities could hire so they wouldn't have to mount these campaigns themselves.

Because of the cost, only a request for monthly donations made sense. As it was, even with monthly donations, a F2F campaign would take a long time to break even.

"Face-to-face became the best practice," said Robert Fox, "but the challenge was that it took 18 months to pay for itself."

Eventually, the face-to-face market also got crowded as scores of canvassers took to the streets. People became tired of being approached for money by eager strangers with clipboards in their hands. In the U.K., F2F canvassers started to become known as "chuggers," a combination of the words "charity" and "mugger."

Special events, always a good stand-by for charity fundraising, but never widely employed by iNGOs because direct marketing had worked so well, was introduced as a way to "engage new audiences."

Oxfam Canada tried a Trailwalker event, where a team navigated a 100 km trail through the course of a weekend and collected pledges for completing it.

"The Trailwalker event had been successful all over the world," Robert Fox said. "In Hong Kong, it was hugely successful. But for whatever reason, in Canada, it didn't work, the reasons for which are hard to determine, even in hindsight."

The ground was shifting underneath the spreadsheet because leveraging money from the public allowed Oxfam to access government funding from CIDA.

"I felt like saying to donors, 'yeah, your dollar is paying for my salary, and get over it...because we're the ones going out there... working with people who are changing the world.' We tried to identify the channels, be honest with the public, but every time there's a 'fly in the eyes' video, it sets you back. It's inuring people to the dignity and power of people."

The success or failure of any channel depends upon cultural consideration in the country where you are operating.

"I'm on the board of Oxfam Mexico," Robert says. "And they are doing face-to-face fundraising in Mexico City. Now, if you think of any city in the world where you don't want to ask strangers for money and where you definitely don't want to take your credit card out on the street, it would be Mexico City. But the program is remarkably successful there. The pitch that's successful is the 'we're tackling inequality here and around the world.' In Mexico City, they get that message."

In a market environment where it's getting more expensive to raise smaller gifts from large numbers of people, the pendulum has swung to raising fewer gifts from smaller groups of people.

There's no smaller group of people than the people involved in what's called philanthrocapitalism, a term popularized by Matthew Bishop, US Business Editor and New York Bureau Chief at *The Economist* magazine and Michael Green, London-based economist and writer who has worked in aid and development, in their book, *Philanthrocapitalism: How the Rich Can Save the World.*

Bishop and Green sum up the role of these philanthropic "hyperagents," big spenders like Bill Gates, Michael Bloomberg and Mark Zuckerberg by saying "the superrich can do things to help solve the world's problems that the traditional power elites in and around government cannot. They are free from the usual pressures that bear down on politicians and activists and company bosses with shareholders to please."

"This democracy deficit is the ghost at the banquet of philanthrocapitalism," said U.S. author, David Rieff, who has written eight books on international affairs (and who, incidentally, is the son of celebrated U.S. writer, Susan Sontag) in his article for *The Nation*, entitled *Philanthrocapitalism: A Self-Love Story*.

"[Bill] Gates has pointed this out himself on many occasions, though his remedy for, as he puts it, not having to 'worry about being voted out at the next election or board meeting' is to 'work hard and to get lots of feedback.'"

Melinda Gates has said, "she and her husband 'learn from their mistakes.'"

One of the mistakes the Gates' have had the opportunity to learn from is the recent attempt by Bill Gates (though his "Coop Dreams" project) to "change the world with chickens." He attempted to donate 100,000 chickens to Bolivia. Bolivia, already having a flourishing poultry industry of its own, rejected the offering and instead demanded an apology.

In the case of Bill and Melinda Gates, 'learning' takes place wholly on their own terms, says Rieff. "And an accountability that's entirely self-imposed and unenforceable by anyone else is not accountability in any serious sense of the term," he writes. "Unlike government development aid, there is literally no check on what Bill and Melinda Gates can do, except their own resources and desires, and no way of making this learning process—when and if it happens—anything more than a voluntary act on their part."

Critics are not welcome.

In 2012, at a televised forum in Australia, Bill Gates dramatically criticized Dambisa Moyo.

"She is an aid critic," he said. "And there's not many because it's moralistically a tough position to take...if you look objectively at what aid has been able to do, you would never accuse it of creating dependency. Having children not die is not creating a dependency.

Having children not be so sick they can't go to school, not having enough nutrition so their brains don't develop — that is not a dependency. That's an evil thing. And books like that are promoting evil."

The motivations of Bill Gates or any other mega-philanthropists are, right now, beside the point.

Their altruistic hearts are making people shudder from one end of the African continent to the other. Because if these guys set their minds on spending money on what they consider are the problems in your neck of the woods, there is no telling where all those good intentions will end up.

10/

Don't Mention the "P" Word

Everyone has something to say about politics.

Groucho Marx called it, "the art of looking for trouble, finding it everywhere, diagnosing it incorrectly and applying the wrong remedies."

Aristotle believed, "democracy is when the indigent, and not the men of property, are the rulers."

A Gandalf Group poll conducted in 2014 for the Ted Rogers School of Management at Ryerson University in Toronto was consistent with other polls regarding trustworthiness of politicians. They led from the bottom at 13 per cent. Only lobbyists scored lower in the rankings at 9 per cent.

Who in their right mind, you might well ask, would want to throw their cap in with that lot?

"With regard to political activities I think there are cultural issues in Canada that need to be gotten over as it relates to charities understanding what impact you have," says charity lawyer, Mark Blumberg.

"A group could have $100 thousand in revenue and could have more impact than a $100 million organization because that group works on an initiative to encourage the government to spend $200 million a year on something."

The Canadian Revenue Agency (CRA) makes allowances for charities to "stand up and say things." Every charity in Canada has the right, under the law, to spend 10 per cent of their resources on political activities. That could include includes activities that "explicitly communicates to the public that a law, policy or decision of any level of government inside or outside Canada should be retained, opposed, or changed."

The allowance for charities to spend money on lobbying and advocacy was recognized in 2002 as part of *A Code of Good Practice on Policy Dialogue*. The code was a part of the *Accord Between the*

Government of Canada and the Voluntary Sector, the result of a wide-ranging Voluntary Sector Initiative. It coincided with the International Year of Volunteers and was signed under the Liberal government of Jean Chrétien.

The code was modeled on a similar arrangement between civil society and government in the U.K. in 1998—the U.K. Compact—and governs political activities and charity.

In Canada the rules are quite clear on the matter.

"The Government of Canada recognizes the need to engage the voluntary sector in open, informed and sustained dialogue in order that the sector may contribute its experience, expertise, knowledge and ideas in developing better public policies and in the design and delivery of programs," the code states.

"Through their dedicated delivery of essential programs, many charities have acquired a wealth of knowledge about how government policies affect people's lives. Charities are well-placed to study, assess, and comment on those government policies. Canadians benefit from the efforts of charities and the practical, innovative ways that they use to resolve complex issues related to delivering social services. Beyond service delivery, their expertise is also a vital source of information for governments to help guide policy decisions. It is therefore essential that charities continue to offer their direct knowledge of social issues to public policy debates."

Political activities permitted by charities, and the ones that need to be expensed within their 10 per cent rule include:
- Buying a newspaper advertisement to pressure the government.
- Organizing a march to Parliament Hill.
- Organizing a conference to support the charity's opinion.

- Hiring a communications specialist to arrange a media campaign.
- Using a mail campaign to urge supporters to contact the government.

The are many activities, however, that are devoted to public policy that the government defines as allowable "charitable activities" including the following scenarios:

- Distributing the charity's research.
- Distributing the research report to election candidates.
- Publishing a research report online.
- Presenting the research report to a Parliamentary Committee.
- Giving an interview about the research report.
- Distributing the research report to all Members of Parliament.
- Participating in an international policy development working group.
- Joining a government advisory panel to discuss policy changes.

Given that there are many issues needing attention, the government's contention that "charities are well-placed to study, assess, and comment on those government policies" and the invitation from government to "help guide policy decisions," one might think Parliament Hill would be crawling with representatives from charities weighed down with ideas and overcome with desire to reduce reliance on food banks, mandate physical education to reduce obesity, put an end to violence against women and prolonged solitary confinement for mentally ill prisoners.

But no.

Charities appear *not* to have received the political activity memo.

Of the $228 billion spent by Canada's 85,000 charities, only $25 million was spent on political activities by about 500 charities in 2014.

To call up the parable of the *Two Men and the Babies*, the amount of money spent on service delivery as opposed dealing with systemic problems means tens of thousands of charities are plucking tens of thousands of crying, drowning babies out of the river. But only .6 per cent of those charities are putting any resources into why the babies are in the water in the first place.

One charity that's decided to run up river is the Canadian Cancer Society and the person leading the charge is Dr. Christine Williams, its Chief of Mission and Scientific Director.

"It depends on how you count it," she says, "but advocacy is about 2 per cent of our expenditures."

"Advocacy is cheap. It's people. It's skilled people and you don't need tons of them, but you need to go with some very good policy analysts in that group. Everything we do as an organization is focused on the biggest bang for the buck. We have the history around tobacco. There's probably not one piece of legislation on tobacco in this country that doesn't have CCS's name on it somewhere. But there's many others issues too. There's pesticides and banning tanning beds for people under 18 years old."

The Canadian Cancer Society's mantra is to "stop cancer before it starts" and its advocacy has demonstrably saved lives. Lung cancer, for example, is the most diagnosed cancer in Canada. But because of new legislation on tobacco use, warnings on cigarette packages, non-smoking by-laws and awareness campaigns—all pieces of legislation fought for by CCS—the incidence of lung cancer among men began to level off in the mid-1980s and has been declining ever since. Since 2006, lung cancer among females is no longer increasing.

"There's a tremendous amount of work that goes into this," says Christine Williams.

"But the question is, because it's so effective and because it's so cheap, and because it actually deals with the systemic issues around cancer prevention — it is an interesting observation to me — there is so little of it that happens."

Given that charities serve the poorest of the poor, the sickest of the sick and the most shunned of all outcasts, who depend on good will to live another day, it feels worse than a missed opportunity.

Whether charities don't feel advocacy is their job or that they don't know how to do it or that they don't understand the rules is cold comfort.

Does lack of action on root causes in Canadian charities point to a sector that doesn't see the self-interest in change?

Some charities argue that they are too poorly resourced to affect systemic change.

"I think it comes down to a broader question of priorities," says Bruce MacDonald, CEO of Imagine Canada. "My observation is that, particularly for mid-size and smaller organizations, they'll pick the service delivery path over the advocacy path…even if…their mission might be greater enhanced if they were to shift the system through some advocacy work. If the choice is 'hire another case worker and deliver programs to 50 more kids' or hire someone to go to Queen's Park or Ottawa to talk about the organization," he says, "guess which path the board of directors and the staff are going to take? The reality…is the service path is the one they're going to pick."

"Charities could spend one thousand times more money on political activities than they say they are spending now on their T3010s," says Mark Blumberg.

If the charity sector spent only ten times more money than they

176

currently say they are spending, it would change the country. So much could be accomplished.

The problem isn't the rules—the 10 per cent limit. Almost no charity is going near that limit. The problem is, according to Blumberg, that charities are not motivated and do not understand the role they can play.

Is the culture of *noblesse oblige,* the idea that the entirety of their moral obligation to "give back" is by taking care of "those less fortunate?" Do they just not see the big picture?

"We're a democratic society. We are very privileged in terms of the sector we have. It does a lot of great work," says Blumberg. "But charities are actually very weak at delivering a lot of things. If you want to really deal with poverty, as a Band-Aid solution, charities are great at it, but if you want to really deal with poverty, you need a political solution."

—•—

In Charles Dickens' *A Christmas Carol,* two gentlemen canvassing for charity pay a visit to Ebenezer Scrooge.

> *"At this festive season of the year, Mr. Scrooge," said the gentleman, taking up a pen, "it is more than usually desirable that we should make some slight provision for the poor and destitute, who suffer greatly at the present time. Many thousands are in want of common necessaries; hundreds of thousands are in want of common comforts, sir."*

"Are there no prisons?" asked Scrooge. "Plenty of prisons," said the gentleman, laying down the pen again. "And the Union workhouses?" demanded Scrooge. "Are they still in operation?"

"They are. Still," returned the gentleman, "I wish I could say they were not."

"The Treadmill and the Poor Law are in full vigour, then?" said Scrooge.

"Both very busy, sir."

"Oh! I was afraid, from what you said at first, that something had occurred to stop them in their useful course," said Scrooge. "I'm very glad to hear it."

"Under the impression that they scarcely furnish Christian cheer of mind or body to the multitude," returned the gentleman, "a few of us are endeavouring to raise a fund to buy the Poor some meat and drink, and means of warmth. We choose this time, because it is a time, of all others, when want is keenly felt, and abundance rejoices. What shall I put you down for?"

"Nothing!" Scrooge replied.

"You wish to be anonymous...?"

"It's not my business," Scrooge returned. "It's enough for a man *to understand his own business, and not to interfere with other people's. Mine occupies me constantly. Good afternoon, gentlemen!"*

While Charles Dickens used Scrooge's lack of charitable inclination to indicate the nature of his doomed soul, he didn't lay the entire charitable pitch at the feet of the wretched poor. He did make the appeal in the broader context of the time. The "Treadmill and the Poor Law are in full vigour," Dickens writes, making the connection between the situation of the marginalized individual within a systemic framework.

Dickens, of course, was familiar with poverty and the treatment of the poor. He had to leave school to work in a factory and his father had been in debtors' prison. While he wrote about the value of charity, he was a vigorous campaigner of children's rights and social reform.

One would imagine if he were running a Canadian charity, he wouldn't shy away from "political activity" that would lessen the suffering of the marginalized people he championed in the 19th century.

———

"We will spend $2.8 million this year on advocacy this year," says Christine Williams about the Canadian Cancer Society. "Not all our advocacy areas are about prevention. We have two or three priorities each year, but one of them right now is palliative care, so that wouldn't fall under prevention at all. We're doing palliative care, tobacco control—always tobacco control (well not always, but this year), research and drug access, that's becoming a big issue."

The Canadian Cancer Society is an exception.

"Unfortunately, it is not a valued part of the work," says Bruce MacDonald, "I think a lot of people say, 'just do the job, feed the homeless or deliver mental health programs but we don't want any of the money we give to you to go towards talking to government. That's lobbying, that's different.'"

Yet nonprofits still hold some sway in the public's mind. For a recent CanTrust Index Survey, Environics Communications talked to Canadians about who they trust for "important information as well as their trust in organizations and leaders to do what is right for Canada and our society." And although Canadians didn't give any information source an unqualified endorsement, nonprofits did come out on top.

	Trust Level
Not-for-profit organizations	59%
News media	54%
Small or medium-sized corporations	44%
Government	40%
Large corporations	29%
None of the above	19%

Figure 10.1: 2016 CanTrust Index, Environics Communications.

"We have both federal and provincial advocacy," clarifies Christine Williams. "I directly oversee our Ottawa staff...that do federal advocacy and work with the federal government. Each province has advocates that work with each provincial government."

"There is a Pan-Canadian advocacy team that coordinates federal and provincial advocacy priorities and they can be slightly different. There can be issues that are hot or pressing for the community in PEI, which might be different from the issues that are pressing in Alberta."

Charities who do lobby government in Ottawa need to register with the Office of the Commissioner of Lobbying of Canada who publishes details of what any registered lobbyist is coming to Ottawa to advocate for, who they are and who they are meeting.

The following list shows what the charities that have opted to engage in political activities are working towards. The nature of the problems they discuss with the federal government bring home the implications of 99.4 per cent of charities ignoring systemic issues and why we are making such little progress in some areas.

Canadian Cancer Society

Palliative and end-of-life care funding to enhance the access and availability of palliative care; Hazardous Products Act, as it relates to the domestic use of asbestos; Health Canada—development of a mandatory reporting system for drug shortages; Income Tax Act, as it relates to the taxation of tobacco companies; Patent Act, as it relates to the use of patents for international humanitarian purposes to address public health problems.

Canadian Council for Refugees

Protection of trafficked persons—advocating for change of Immigration and Refugee Protection Act to guarantee temporary and permanent protection for trafficked persons; The Federal-Provincial Fiscal Arrangements Act, with respect to the 2015 amendment allowing provinces to impose minimum residency requirements on newly arrived refugee claimants.

Canadian Diabetes Association

Aboriginal Diabetes Initiative—work towards making funding for this Initiative permanent. (Previous work directed towards continuation of funding beyond 2010); Change the Disability Tax Credits to cover chronic diseases; Increase Federal funding for Diabetes Research—work directed towards increasing funding to federal granting councils, in particular CIHR through the Federal Budget; Increase funds for diabetes in the Federal Budget specifically to increase funds directed to the Canadian Diabetes Strategy to reflect growth in diabetes prevalence and cost.

Canadian HIV/AIDS Legal Network

An Act to amend the Patent Act and the Food and Drugs Act (The Jean Chretien Pledge to Africa), S.C. 2004, c.23 Lobbying related to amendments aimed at simplifying further use of the act; Corrections and Conditional Release Act, S.C. 1992, c.20 Our interest is in ensuring that this legislation facilitates access to prevention information tools and services on the Human Immunodeficiency Virus (HIV), and facilitates access to adequate care, treatment and support for prisoners with HIV; Criminal Code R.S.C. 1985, C-46 Our interest is in ensuring that this law and its application in practice does not impede access to prevention information, tools and services (for example needle exchange programs, supervised injection facilities, methadone treatment) on the Human Immunodeficiency (HIV) and other health services for people who use drugs.

Family Service Toronto

Child Poverty — Seeking further commitment and funding to reduce child poverty.

Heart and Stroke Foundation of Canada

Expand federal infrastructure programs to include active transportation infrastructure; Extend the indirect costs of research program to include health charity funded research; Implementation of policies and programs to make healthy food affordable and accessible for all Canadians; Close loopholes on flavoured tobacco products; expand tobacco packaging health warnings; Implement a monitoring mechanism to track food and industry progress on sodium reduction; Implement regulations to restrict industry marketing of foods and beverages to children and youth; Improve nutrition labeling regulations, including nutrition facts tables; That the federal government allocates resources to fund research related to heart disease and stroke and programs to prevent dementia; Introduce trans fat regulations to limit the level of trans fats in processed foods; Implement a levy on manufacturers of beverages high in free sugars (energy dense, nutrient poor). This levy should be an excise tax and be based on free sugars per unit. Revenues from such a taxation stream should be used to subsidize vegetables and fruit to make healthy eating more affordable.

Médecins Sans Frontières (MSF)

Obtain contributions from the Department of Global Affairs Canada for the delivery of medical humanitarian assistance in specific geographies; Discuss ongoing operational issues in relation to the delivery of humanitarian aid in specific geographies.

Right to Play

Obtain contributions from Global Affairs Canada for the delivery of development and humanitarian programming for each of the following countries: Benin, Burundi, China, Ethiopia, Ghana, Jordan, Lebanon, Liberia, Mali, Mozambique, Pakistan, the Palestinian Territories (West Bank and Gaza), Rwanda, Tanzania, Thailand and Uganda; Obtain contributions from Indigenous and Northern Affairs Canada and Health Canada for the delivery of programming in Canada; Discuss the prioritization of children and youth's well-being, development and protection with Global Affairs Canada and Federal Government Official; Discuss the prioritization of children and youth's well-being, development and protection with Indigenous and Northern Affairs Canada, Health Canada and Federal Government Officials.

United Church of Canada

Canada's international trade policy and international development policy with respect to mining in El Salvador and Guatemala; Canada's international trade policy and international development policy with respect to mining in Africa in general terms. No discussion of any particular proposal, bill, program, regulation, policy or program; Labeling of Israeli settlement goods entering Canada; and support for exclusion of settlement products from Canada-Israeli Free Trade Agreement.

World Wildlife Federation (WWF)

Communicated with respect to COP21 and the essential elements of a global climate agreement, that ultimately should be implemented through a clear policy and regulatory pathway for achieving CO_2 reductions by 2020 and beyond; Communicated with respect to the Green Budget Coalition's Vision for environmental leadership in the 2016 Budget; discussed recommendations for environment, climate, energy, industry, fisheries, aboriginal affairs, and marine and terrestrial protected areas; Communicated with respect to the validity of Shell exploration permits in Lancaster Sound and the designation of Lancaster Sound as a National Marine Conservation Area.

Charities don't have to be big to have a voice. The Canadian Council for Refugees, which is lobbying for the protection of trafficked persons, had a budget of just over $400,000 in 2014. The Canadian HIV/AIDS Legal Network, with revenue of $1.5 million in 2014, is advocating for improved access to HIV/AIDS prevention information and access to adequate care, treatment and support for prisoners with HIV.

A charity also doesn't have to be a national organization in order to lobby. Family Service Toronto, a community-based group providing all sorts of crisis services for families in the city, are working on the issue of child poverty in Ottawa, something they clearly know a lot about.

Many Canadians scratch their heads in bewilderment at why we are not making more progress on social issues. We put a great deal of money into health and social welfare, yet never seem to get ahead.

Part of the answer might lie in the fact that the organizations charged by society to provide services to the sick and marginalized are not talking. The voices of marginalized people are absent from the public discourse and one would think that charities would be a natural source for their perspective.

When the Canadian government made its pact with the voluntary sector in 2002, it said, "many charities have acquired a wealth of knowledge about how government policies affect people's lives. Charities are well-placed to study, assess, and comment on those government policies."

Judging the sector on that benchmark alone suggests a less than passing grade.

The question is who—if not the charities funded to do the day-to-day work around serious health and social issues are not stepping up to the plate to address root causes of problems—is responsible for giving marginalized and sick people a voice?

"Distribution Should Undo Excess, and Each Man Have Enough"

King Lear: Act 4, Scene 1

Inequity seems as fixed to life on earth as earth, wind, air and fire.

We understand that there is enough food and wealth to sustain us all. The matter of who gets what is the rub.

In 1906 Italian economist Vilfredo Pareto created a mathematical formula to quantify his observations about the unequal distribution of land. His calculation rounded to twenty percent of people owning eighty percent of the wealth. His theory became known as the Pareto Principle and he based his findings on statistics from British income, findings further replicated in studies of Paris and Prussia.

Pareto also gave some thought to the optimal allocation of resources and calculated a mathematical formula where resources were allocated most efficiently when "one party's situation cannot be improved without making the other party's situation worse."

The theory, called Pareto's Efficiency, used mathematical models to study conflict and cooperation and to codify the idea that "rational and reasonable" people might not cooperate with each other even if it is in both their best interests to do so.

His model has wide-ranging application in economics, as well as engineering and social science, in particular in game theory. The "prisoners dilemma" is a longstanding example of game theory.

It takes two prisoners, gang members, who are charged with a serious crime, let's say armed robbery. They are both being questioned separately and have no communication with each other. It is clear to both, from their lawyers, the prosecution doesn't have enough evidence to convict them on a charge of armed robbery, which comes with a sentence of five years. But, they are told, the authorities do have evidence to convict them on a lesser charge, which would put them behind bars for less than a year. What is their choice of action? In the game, there is no retribution waiting for them outside.

If Prisoner One decides to betray Prisoner Two on the armed robbery charge but Prisoner One stays silent, Prisoner One might go free for turning state witness and Prisoner Two would get a five year sentence, or vice versa.

If Prisoner One decides to betray Prisoner Two and Prisoner Two does the same to Prisoner One, then they both get a five-year sentence.

If they both decide to say nothing, they each spend less than one year in jail.

The betrayal strategy could be of the most benefit to an individual prisoner, but only if the other prisoner does not also employ the betrayal strategy. If they both opt for the betrayal strategy, they both end up serving a longer prison sentence. Saying nothing also has risk because you could be the one that gets betrayed and you've behaved like a sitting duck. The silent strategy will guarantee you will serve a sentence in prison even if it is a shorter one but depends on the expectation of cooperation from the other side.

Game theory is used to define some of the underpinnings of nuclear disarmament, as well as providing a theoretical idea for keeping capitalism sustainable and in check; it all works out okay as long as one party doesn't abuse the trust of the other.

There is an increasingly vocal group of critiques that say rampant capitalism in some quarters has done just that.

In today's world Pareto's 80/20 rule seems a quaint holdover from the Franklin Roosevelt's post–war New Deal. The Occupy Principle rules this millennium, where 99 per cent of the world's wealth is controlled by 1 per cent of the world's population. Political and religious leaders throughout the world are concerned about the increasing gap between the rich and poor and some counties, including Europe, are roiling messes because of it.

President Barack Obama has described rising income inequality as the "defining challenge of our time" and often repeated his message that inequality has increased across the developed world.

Pope Francis wrote in the *Joy of the Gospel,* his first papal *exhortation,* emphasized the subjects of exclusion and inequality. In the hierarchy of Vatican communications, an *exhortation* is one step below a formal encyclical but one step above *a letter to the faithful.*

"How can it be," he wrote, "that it is not a news item when an elderly homeless person dies of exposure, but it is news when the stock market loses two points?"

"Of course, the poor have long been with us, and Catholic priests and lay workers the world over have long made great exertions on their behalf," staff writer, John Cassidy, was moved to write in his *New Yorker essay, Pope Francis's Challenge To Global Capitalism* in December 2013. "All too often, though, this charitable work has coexisted with a Church hierarchy that studiously avoided critiquing the political and economic system that generates poverty and inequality."

Yet Roman Catholic Church is not alone in its avoidance of the critique of a system that generates inequality.

If we were to use increased equity among world citizens as a benchmark of the success of charitably tending to the world's wounded, we must acknowledge the charity model as a complete failure. As it exists today, charity is preserving inequity both at home and abroad as if it was peaches in a jam jar.

"But that's like the idea of democracy being a failure until we look at other forms of government," said Tennys Hanson, CEO of Toronto General and Western Hospital Foundation. Maybe so, but the critique of democracy has been well and often written about since the days of the city-state in Athens. And remarkably, given the resources expended by charities and the lives it holds in its benevolent arms, the charitable sector has remained blithely beyond critique.

One quick word search of "democracy" at Amazon.com revealed 79,924 available titles on the subject. Using "charitable sector" as a search term on Amazon.com revealed 87 available titles.

It is difficult to know how the sector would bear up under scrutiny because there has been so little of it. But if we held it up to the same "empirical study of results" as is currently employed in developing countries, we might get a clearer picture of how well the West is doing on its own problems. And we might, for example, look at studies such as the *Child and youth injury prevention: A public health approach* (2012) from the Canadian Paediatric Society. That piece of research would tell us that:

- Unintentional injury has been described as the "neglected disease of modern society," an "invisible epidemic," and "the principal public health problem in (North) America today."
- In Canada, injury is the leading cause of death for not only children, but for all Canadians between the ages of one and 44.
- According to the WHO, if high-income countries were to implement programs using proven effective interventions, which considered the special vulnerability of children, more than a thousand children's lives would be saved each day.
- Injury prevention, like immunization, has the potential to be among the greatest public health achievements of the 21st century.

The leading causes of death among Canadians one to 19 years of age is shown in Table 11.1. (The table doesn't include 838 children who die from congenital conditions, short gestation or maternal complications in the first year of life.)

Cause of Death	Number of Children	Percentage Among Top Four Causes
Accidents (unintentional injuries)	624	57.6%
Suicide (intentional self-harm)	218	20.1%
Malignant neoplasms	195	18.0%
Congenital conditions	47	4.3%
Total	1084	100.0%

Figure 11.1

Given the empirical evidence around injury prevention, one might think that charities interested in the health of children would take it upon themselves to invest in, or lobby government to invest in, as the Canadian Paediatric Society says, "proven effective interventions" that could save children's lives each day. (Canada ranks 18 out of 25 Organization for Economic Co-operation and Development, OECD, countries by this measure.)

Or people might turn their attention to children who are living in the child welfare system. The Children's Aid Foundation of Canada (CAF) uses "child welfare" as a technical term to describe, "a set of government and private services designed to protect children and encourage family stability."

The main aim of these services is to safeguard children from abuse and neglect.

Status of Children	Number	Notes
Living in foster and group homes	76,000	That represents 1% of the nation's child population who are living in foster care, group homes, or with family members in formal kinship care arrangements as a result of the abuse or neglect they have suffered at the hands of their caregivers.
At risk in the community	250,000	These are children who are receiving support and services from child protection agencies while living with their families in the community. These children are often at risk of experiencing abuse, neglect and extreme poverty.
Transitioning out of care	2,300	These young people "age out" of the child welfare system every year upon turning 18 or 19 and are forced to face the overwhelming task of establishing their independence with little to no financial or emotional support.
Total	328,300	

Figure 11.2: Children in Child Welfare System (Children's Aid Foundation).

The CAF is currently running a $60 million national campaign to supplement the funds government is devoting to the care of these 328,300 children and youth.

Valerie McMurtry, whose career has included leadership roles at the Canadian Olympic Foundation, Holland Bloorview Kids Rehabilitation Hospital Foundation and the Mount Sinai Hospital Foundation, currently leads the Children's Aid Foundation and says the major challenges for raising the $60 million they need to support children in care is the fact that the children are invisible. As the most legally "protected" children in Canada, we can't see their needs. There is also stigma involved in the way people look at children in the child welfare system.

"People say 'I raised my children, why can't they raise theirs?'" according to McMurtry, "but in the child welfare system there are larger issues at play including poverty and mental illness." McMurtry says that, "on average, a child in the 'system' will change families five times in their childhood." It's hard to know how anyone — child or adult — would emerge from that experience intact.

It is perhaps unsurprising that the national high school graduation rates for children in the child welfare system hover around 33 per cent. The national average for high school graduation in Canada is 85 per cent.

After two years, the CAF campaign has raised $27.5 million.

———

According to the Public Health Agency of Canada (PHAC), 880 children under the age of 15 are diagnosed with cancer each year. The incidence has remained stable since 1992, but survival has improved. PHAC project 150 children will die from the disease in a year.

Leukemia is the most commonly occurring type of cancer at affecting 290 children; cancer of the brain or nervous system cancers are next with affecting 176 children and lymphomas are the third most common cancer affecting 97 children.

The improvement in leukemia survival rates has come as a result of a tremendous amount of money devoted to bio-medical research. And hundreds of millions of dollars more continue to pour into laboratory research for the life-threatening children's illnesses that killed 242 children in 2008.

Sick Kids Hospital Foundation in Toronto made the decision it needed $400 million to build a research institute to further these research goals, a great many of which involve cancer research, to accommodate "the most specialized research and learning needs." They will spend about another $60 million a year to keep the lights on, pay staff, cover the capital costs and take care of general upkeep.

Whether the lack of a 750,000 square foot research facility was a priority problem that needed fixing or the desire of wealthy donors, we don't know. There was not wider community consultation about the needs of Canadian children prior to the research facility being built. The charity made the decision, all three levels of government dutifully contributed to it, another $100 million was raised from donors and $200 million was raised in financing that the Foundation will pay the interest on.

Let's recall the words of Dr. Cindy Gauvreau who, in Chapter 4 — *Our Cancer Future,* said, "In the gold standard of decision-making processes, you want the decision to be made for as many people as possible. So if the question is whether you are going to fund a drug that's fantastically expensive and lifesaving but only gives you five lives" she explained as an example, "as opposed to paying for a vaccine program for HPV, for cervical cancer, oral cancer that is going to affect a far larger number of people. That's the balance that has to be met."

Are we applying the "gold standard of decision-making" in the charitable sector when we have a children's health charities sector that's focuses hundreds of millions of dollars on the third and fourth leading causes of death among children?

At the same time, very few charities exist to highlight and raise money for the first and second causes of childhood deaths — unintentional accidents, a vast majority of which could be prevented says the Canadian Pediatric Association, and suicide?

Prevention is the key, says Valerie McMurtry. The best way

to stop children from ending up in the child welfare system is to provide the mother and the family with the support—both material and emotional—at the earliest stages of a child's life. It is at this stage when we can most successfully focus our prevention resources.

It is not unusual for an infant to be removed from her mother's care if, for example, mom doesn't have the proper crib or equipment deemed needed to keep the child safe. And depending on the families' background, the new mom might need a great deal of emotional and social support in order to cope.

While we might spend hundreds of thousands of dollars on a newborn who needs a new lung or open heart surgery—and fundraise for that with gusto and slick marketing campaigns—what makes us so reluctant to invest in other children, who may not be physical ill, but at risk in other ways? How is it that we can have such deep empathy for one child, but turn our backs on another that's born under difficult circumstances? What does that say about the value we place on the lives of children who are living in the child welfare system and opposed to children in a hospital?

Empirical evidence and the "gold standard of decision-making" are not compatible with the path the charity model is leading us down.

It is time to ask the serious questions around who is steering the charities regarding where the majority of the sector's resources are spent and where the pea-sized brain of the sector dinosaur—thumping its way around the country, impenetrable and with no understanding of its own strength—is blindly leading us now?

The amount of money funneled through the charitable sector has doubled in the last decade. Yet every charity operates as a separate entity with little awareness of what a charity across town, let alone the country and the world is doing.

The result is an overall lack of progress on important issues.

Despite individual success stories by some groups such as the Canadian Cancer Research Alliance, cancer research in Canada as a whole cannot be fully surveilled or prioritized because not all the players who raise and spend cancer research funds will cooperate in sharing that information.

Regardless of evidence pointing to its effectiveness, only 10 per cent of cancer research resources are focused on prevention.

Ninety-five per cent of all cancer resources are spent in the developed world.

Powerful charities — primarily hospitals and universities — have adopted a "no holds barred" approach in the amount of resources they are willing to expend to ensure their position at the top of the market and they don't see any reason why they shouldn't raise the money to build new buildings and endow their continued wealth far into the future.

The same conditions that cause the widening gap in income inequality in society generally are replicated in the charitable sector. Those that have the money think their cause is the one most entitled to it.

There is an ingrained stratification of the charitable sector where causes such as biomedical research (represented by the few) resides at the top of a resource hierarchy, investing hundreds of millions of dollars while sitting on hundreds of millions of reserves. At the bottom of the resource hierarchy are community-based charities (represented by the many), with very little money to invest in fund-raising and none of the security offered by reserves.

—•—

Charities are under no obligation to do the best thing for the largest number of people.

The demonstrable needs of a marginalized people are not what guides charity. A charity guides its own actions, acting as a self-contained ecosystem, with the choice of having a broad view or a narrow view of its responsibilities. There is no obligation on the part of a charity to deal at all with what brought unfortunate people to their door, and they, by the rate at which they undertake political activity, do not don the mantel of social change easily.

With lack of surveillance of the sector impacts and the pre-occupation by sector leaders and "evaluators" on manufactured issues like administrative costs, it appears there are a good many people who would like to keep status quo.

Most charities operate with an almost singular focus on the tasks in front of them on any given day. The goal of creating a better Band-Aid and solving the presenting problem rather than preventing it in the first place guides most charities. They don't visualize themselves as the ones responsible for figuring out what brought you to them. Nor do the vast majority look for issues outside their mission to where people might be falling through the cracks.

Consider the outbreak of skin rashes and lesions at Kashechewan First Nations in March 2016 among babies and toddlers that looked so bad news outlets carrying pictures of their sweet little faces disfigured by crusted red and green sores and lesions, carried a graphic image trigger warning. Their eyes, wide and round with innocence had no understanding of what was happening to them or why.

Sixteen of these little children, so badly infected by noxious sores, were airlifted to hospital. That hospital, a designated charity, run by a volunteer board of directors with an indeterminate understanding of broad-based health issues, and funded from a provincial government coffers, will be able to — or not able to — treat the children and send them back home. They don't have any responsibility to get to the bottom of what's happening with these children. That's outside their mandate.

Judging by its funding priorities, the cancer research community doesn't appear to be too enthusiastic about people "*not* taking that cancer journey." Their research funding decisions indicate they would prefer to deal with the disease when it's full blown.

Reluctance to fund studies on contaminants in the air, water and soil has driven world-renowned population research scientist, Dr. Louise Parker, to the brink. When we visited her in *Chapter Four*—she'd said she'd "had enough" and was retiring because of the "lack of expert review and scarcity of funding" for her prevention work around arsenic, a Class One carcinogen.

"Prevention research doesn't involve fancy-dancy laboratories," she said. "Prevention involves people, not patients, and who wants to pay for them?"

The reluctance of the charitable sector to look at systemic issues is costing our governments and economies billions of dollars without improving the health and well-being of the people who need their support.

The citizens of developing countries are helpless against our good works. By its very nature, the way charity is administered in developing countries is patronizing. It is standard operating procedure for iNGOs to engage local partners, all to determine what *we* think *their* need is. Funding to iNGOs from the Canadian International

Development Agency (CIDA) depends on the Canadian charity having direct control of the project.

Some organizations do this work with a greater degree of sensitivity to the power imbalance than others, but the underlying premise of the exchange is the same. One of the people in this exchange knows what is good for you. And it isn't you.

All this while governments pump aid money into the governments of developing countries that will, for one, ensure the recipient countries will not have to put themselves to the task of developing their own tax base and therefore be accountable to their own people. This ensures that there is enough pooling money at the top of the food chain to make it worthwhile for war lords, religious zealots and the power hungry to whip up any kind of conflict they can that will bring them closer to grabbing the keys to the vault.

Against this backdrop, hundreds of thousands of men, women and children in vulnerable positions fall precipitously into the deadly chasm of famine and war that's opening up beneath their feet. Humanitarian aid workers, unarmed and unshielded, rush in at great risk to their own lives, hopeful they can prevent a few people from hitting the bottom of the widening abyss.

Talk to any humanitarian aid worker and they'll tell you how well that battle is going.

Enter Bill Gates with a anti-malaria bed net in his hand and a reading group from Rockaway who has decided to visit a Kenyan village in order to distribute school books and you'll have a cover shot for *Charity Today*.

—•—

Inequity is ingrained in the sector itself.

Tax incentives serve to etch this inequity onto the canvas of the sector. In the charity world, rich donors get more of a tax break than less wealthy donors. Wealthy donors can set an organization's priorities.

Charities are, by and large, the implementers of social programs across the country and an important means by which citizens can engage in strengthening the social fabric. By taking part in meaningful volunteer work they also express their inherent values.

Some charities, like hospital foundations and universities, have lots of money. Organizations with a small charitable footprint—organizations that are often dealing with stigmatized or marginalized issues—don't.

The charity model leaves the people they exist to serve hanging in the breech.

First, Do No Harm

The charitable sector is a bulwark protecting the status quo.

It keeps full-fledged poverty and social unrest at bay. It nurses fevered brows and feeds hungry people but, as evidenced by the 99.4 per cent of charities who take no action to deal with the systemic problems that drive people to their doorstep, the sector does not have the temperament to lead anyone into revolution.

Since the 17th century, charities have laid the blame of infirmity at the feet of the infirm and have done so with the satisfaction of "helping those less fortunate" and remaining head and shoulders above the fray.

In its present state, charity is ill-equipped to deliver us from the problems of today.

It is safe to say that charity also entrenches inequity.

At its worst, charity acts as a cipher for people who argue, "Governments need to get out of the business of looking after people," even as it structurally provides the most lucrative benefits to its richest benefactors and receives 65 per cent of its revenue from government sources.

Charities make decisions that can be in the best interest of their constituency, decisions that could also run counter to the best interests of the majority of the Canadian public. The control of $246 billion of government funding, self-generated revenue and charitable donations is in the hands of the boards of directors of charitable organizations that continue to operate, by and large, without public scrutiny. Every day, thousands of lives are held in the palm of charities' hands and although it is the second largest sector in the economy, it has successfully hidden behind the fairy dust of good intentions.

Charity has not been at the forefront of any broad-based social movement of the 20th or 21st century. Neither the quest for civil rights, women's rights, pay equity, LGBTQ rights, the anti-war movement, the environmental movement or the "silent spring" was launched from the charitable sector.

Neither has bio-medical research, where so many charitable dollars end up, been the source of the major medical advancements that have given us the longer, healthier lives we lead.

The most significant advances in our general health, which has added 25 years to our life span, have been made possible by public health initiatives, not disease-based research. Even in the areas where charities have made a difference — anti-smoking, drunk driving and food labeling legislation — have only happened when charities engaged in political activity, which we know 99.4 per cent of charities reject.

"To hell with charity," famed community organizer, Saul Alinsky said. "The only thing you get is what you are strong enough to get — so you had better organize." Mr. Alinksy believed that community organizing was how to improve living conditions.

Here are the 12 greatest public health achievements according to the Public Health Agency of Canada (PHAC):

- Acting on the social determinants of health (such as income, education, early childhood development and social connections).
- Control of infectious diseases.
- Decline in deaths from coronary heart disease and stroke (through eating better, exercise).
- Family planning.
- Healthier environments (flouride in water for example).
- Healthier mothers and babies.
- Motor-vehicle safety.
- Recognition of tobacco use as a health hazard.

- Safer and healthier foods.
- Safer workplaces.
- Universal policies (income maintenance, health care).
- Vaccination.

If we expect charities to lead the charge on the pressing issues of today—issues like the vast movements of refugees, climate change, violence against women, mental health, homelessness, obesity, poverty, or racism—the evidence indicates that we, with few exceptions, will be disappointed.

Based on the unprecedented amounts of money going into the charitable sector to deliver social programs, one would think there is room for charities to be a bigger part of the solution to those problems. Yet, all the evidence suggests that the catalysts will not come from the sector itself.

The existing leadership group, one of which is Imagine Canada, is only motivated to deal with technical issues such as tax incentives and charity "standards" that mostly revolve around balance sheet issues. Their mandate is cheerleading and finding ways to encourage people—especially wealthy people—to give more money. Fundraising professionals, who are also organized into an association, focus on fundraising how-to workshops and providing the environment for fundraisers to get a professional designation, the Certified Fund Raising Executive (CFRE).

These groups are not likely the ones to wake up one morning, see the bus running over them and exclaim 'Now I get it!'

In order for the sector to become more effective and accountable—and even if the humanitarian argument holds no sway, there are 246 billion other reasons to do this—three areas need to be addressed. They are three pillars of our society—the media, government and charities themselves.

1. **The news media is going to have to start covering the sector like it covers business or politics, with knowledgeable reporters who know what to look for, understand the dynamics, follow the leadership changes and most importantly, follow the money.**

People often suggest that charities should be "run like a business." It makes no sense, of course. Charities have nothing to do with making a profit. Their notional success is measured in human terms. They need to be better managed, yes, but run like a business, no.

They do, however, if only for the amounts of money involved—and regardless of its impacts on people—need to be reported on like business or politics because today's charities, with huge amounts of government and corporate money flowing through them, are the offspring of both.

Adequate media coverage will make a difference—in big ways and small.

Recently, news coverage by the *Globe and Mail* changed how one small Canadian charity operates.

In the spring of 2016, the paper ran a story about a charity called Canada Company that offers scholarships to "fallen soldiers" and revealed that the scholarship committee turned down an application from the family of a soldier, a captain, who had served in the military for 33 years and did four tours of Afghanistan. He had suffered from debilitating

PTSD before ultimately taking his own life. He was one of 62 known soldiers and veterans who killed themselves after returning from Afghanistan.

In an email from the Canada Company president, the mother was told her two children were not eligible for an education fund because the circumstances of her husband's death did not meet the organization's scholarship criteria.

The family was devastated by the response from Canada Company. Despite repeated requests over six weeks, the *Globe and Mail* reported that no members of the scholarship committee were available to comment, but the scholarship committee's decision was "fully supported by the charity's board of directors."

Ultimately, Canada Company changed their minds and their policy. The family said it was the media attention that made them do it.

Comprehensive and analytical media coverage of charity is the exception.

In June, 2016 a huge charity story played out on the European front when Médecins Sans Frontières (MSF) announced it would "no longer take funds from the European Union and Member States, in opposition to their damaging deterrence policies and intensifying attempts to push people and their suffering away from European shores."

The issue that brought MSF to the breaking point was the refugee deal the EU worked out with Turkey. The multi-billion euro financial aid package was payment if Turkey would keep the refugees within their borders.

"We have been treating victims of Europe's deterrence approach to migration for years, in what has become an acute humanitarian crisis on European soil," MSF said in its statement. "We've reset bones broken by police, treated children shot in the head by rubber bullets and rinsed the eyes of babies doused in tear gas. Instead of focusing on alleviating the crisis, EU and Member States have decided to simply walk away and push it on to others."

MSF made the dramatic decision to refuse aid after the European Commission unveiled a proposal to "replicate the EU-Turkey logic across more than 16 countries in Africa and the Middle East." These deals would impose trade and development aid cuts on countries that do not stem migration to Europe or facilitate forcible returns and reward those that do.

There are been some criticism of the position taken by MSF accusing them of hurting refugees by not taking the money. But the reality is that MSF is making a stand that it is not an extension of its donor country's political priorities. It is a *nongovernmental* organization.

If such a stand had been taken by some of the aid groups who were involved in South Somalia in the year before the

2011 famine—a famine that was constructed by donor countries that said they were enacting their anti-terrorist policy—200,000 people may not have died of starvation.

Yet MSF's declaration has not been widely covered.

Instead, what is being covered are stories like the one *Global News* reported on in June 2016, *"Women and children to benefit from historic $54M gift to the University of Alberta."* Nowhere did the story specify *how* women and children would benefit beyond vague references to "research developments," "recruiting international-calibre researchers" and acting as "an incubator for research." The colour in the piece was a story about a woman carrying triplets, one of who would require high tech open-heart surgery as soon as he was born.

Also, no information was given about the time frame in which the money would be spent. If it was an endowment, the most likely scenario, it would have been helpful to know the percentage of the annual payout. A 3.5 per cent payout is $1.89 million a year, 4.5 per cent payout is $2.43 million a year and the principal of $54 million will sit in an investment account until the end of time or, at least, the end of banking, as we know it.

No clearer message could be sent about the institutionalization of activities to promote the health of women and children, a pressing public policy issue in this country.

Yet, it's not a failure of *Global News* per se. Media outlets all over the world, outlets that would be embarrassed to give business such gushing endorsements, are guilty of being the chief thank-you letter writers to wealthy donors.

The *New York Times Review of Books* published an article, *Covering the One Percent,* in January 2016 detailing how media outlets *could* cover charities, especially the activities of high net worth donors. Like in Canada, U.S. taxpayers subsidize charitable giving. It's estimated that $40 billion is diverted from the U.S public treasury through charitable donations each year.

When donors approach a nonprofit, the article says, they are more likely to say "here's what I'd like to do, here's my agenda," not "how can I help you?" Mainstream news organizations haven't caught on to this new activism.

2. **The federal government needs to fund a mechanism through which the charitable sector can get a grip on its relationship to government and broader public policy goals.**

In the early 2000's a pact between what was then called the National Voluntary Initiative and the Canadian government was signed. It was called *A Code of Good Practice on Policy Dialogue.*

In *A Short History of Voluntary Sector-Government Relations in Canada,* Peter T. Elson documents the path that led to the signing of the accord. In 2000, the federal government funded a Voluntary Sector Initiative (VSI) and Phase One came with $96.6 million for five years. Its birth was heralded in the Speech from the Throne. The initiative would consult the sector on seven areas of interest—capacity, regulation, vision and underlying principles, regulations, the sector's contribution to Canadian society, technological needs, and coordination and oversight.

The signed accord set out guiding principles of the voluntary sector/government partnership, provided a framework for public policy dialogue and good practices for the sector. In 2002, both parties agreed on commitments to action.

The commitment of the voluntary sector at that time was to:

- Continue to identify important or emerging issues and trends in communities, and act on them or bring them to the attention of the Government of Canada; and
- Serve as a means for the voices and views of all parts of the voluntary sector to be represented to and heard by the Government of Canada, ensuring that the full depth and diversity of the sector is reached and engaged.

From 2003–2005, some of the recommendations from Phase One were implemented, and reforms for registered charities were made, but by the end of 2005, the federal government was on an election footing and, as the new Conservative government came to power, the political will behind the project was lost. The sector also lost the will to claim the territory that went with its stated responsibility to bring issues to the attention of government.

In the intervening decade, charity leadership walked away from substantive public policy debate and engaged in a technical dialogue about percentages of administrative costs, a donors' "bill of rights" and tax incentives.

The vacuum was filled by organizations like Charity Navigator in the U.S. and Charity Intelligence in Canada that used the same technical criteria as charity leaders talked about themselves. Many in the sector have struggled against that bridle, but by and large, most charities willingly adopted the criteria as an adequate benchmark of their work and sought out the blessings of the self-styled evaluators.

In order for charities to use their resources more effectively, substantive public policy debate on the *issues* charities are dealing with needs to be re-ignited in all western countries.

In Canada specifically, the updating of the signed accord between the National Voluntary Sector and the federal government in 2002 could serve as the starting point for a modern-day pact, just as the U.K. did with *The U.K. Compact* that was developed in 1998 and updated in 2010. At least it was developed before misguided technical criteria took hold and still has some flavor of the "common good" about it.

The question of *who* might represent the charitable sector in such an endeavor is a thorny one, but the most productive course of action would be to have people who have an understanding of the sector *as a whole*, both domestically and internationally, as opposed to people who represent one aspect of the sector and who would (such is human nature) try to create an environmental to further enhance their position.

If, and it's a big if, charities can begin to grapple with the issues at hand, some of which have been outlined in this book, we might be able to begin the shift to a Canadian charitable sector that is dynamic, problem-solving and equitable as opposed to one that is largely moribund, hand-cuffed to the status quo and, increasingly, a tax haven and "intellectual capture" opportunity for the wealthy.

The biggest obstacle is the charities themselves.

3. **Charities, especially boards of directors, need to take a good, long and honest look at what they are doing, not only in relation to statistics such as "people served," but also in regards to what they are doing to address those systemic issues bringing people to their door.**

In the 21st century, with all the communications and research tools at our disposal, there has never been a time when information is more accessible. Charities must understand where they sit in their community, municipality, province, territory, country and globally. It is the responsibility of each and every charity, who all receive generous support from the Canadian taxpayer, to understand their issues.

We are counting on people who are working on the frontline to bring this insight. Their ability to articulate, and act on, the experience of their clients is a measure of their effectiveness.

Charities must engage in political activities and public awareness work so we can learn from their experience and make changes in the way our society works. It is another measure of effectiveness.

Charities need to acknowledge the support they receive from the citizens of their city, province, territory or country. To not do so diminishes that commitment and presents an unfinished picture of where "tax dollars" go, making it easier for politicians to place a strangle-hold on revenue sources for services. That is a measurement of effectiveness.

As public institutions, charities need to understand that they are accountable to the public. If the media, government and charities themselves each do their part, there is an opportunity to use the tremendous amount of resources—$246 billion, greater than the GDP of most countries on earth—for its maximum effectiveness, especially as it relates to making sure Canadian children and the most marginalized among us have the opportunities they need to succeed.

But the charitable sector—whether because it believes it is on the right side of its god or that good intentions are an end to itself—is being held back by tunnel vision, hubris and some kind of weird notion of its own victimization.

More often than not, critique of the charitable sector is met with a defensive response. "We're doing our best!" "Everyone here means well!" "The government is just not giving us enough money!" "We're just doing what the donor wants!"

"How are we supposed to know all that stuff? We're just a charity!"

In the new world of open and modern-day charity work, this will not be acceptable.

A progressive forward-thinking charity will see its work clearly, understand what it can do, see itself in relation to others, make decisions according to externalized criteria and be prepared to answer for those decisions.

— · —

A couple of years ago I was meeting with a prospective donor, a retired industrialist who had made his money in steel. A down-to-earth guy, he said he was new to the "charity game." He told me he had spent a lifetime making money and now that he was retired, he wanted to give some of it away.

I asked him which he found more difficult—making money or giving it away.

"Giving it away is more difficult," he said, "hands down. Because the first thing you have to make sure of is that you are not making things worse."

He knows money, in and of itself, doesn't have any inherent worthiness. It depends entirely on what you do with it and that bad things can come from the best of intentions.

About the Author

Gail Picco is a strategist and nonprofit executive who has worked in the sector for 25 years, most of which as President of Gail Picco Associates. She is currently Principal with The Osborne Group in Toronto. Prior to starting Gail Picco Associates, she worked in a shelter for assaulted women and children for eight years. She is the author of *What the Enemy Thinks,* a recent novel set in the nonprofit sector; *And Then I Said,* a "best-of" blog collection, and *Your Working Girl,* a blog of memoir and commentary on politics, charity and popular culture. Gail also writes a regular column, *Going Deeper,* for *Hilborn Charity News.*

Acknowledgements

In the course of researching this book, I have met dozens of hugely smart people with a lot to say. I want to especially thank Kim Badovinac, my guide through the cancer research maze, and other cancer specialists including Dr. Paul Demers, Dr. Cindy Gauvreau, Dr. Louise Parker, Dr. Luca Pisterzi and Dr. Christine Williams, all of whom were extremely helpful. The book wouldn't have been possible without you. Brock Warner from War Child recounted his time in South Sudan more than he probably cared to. My admiration for him and his colleagues grew with each recounting. Robert Fox was frank and forthright. I appreciate that. Hospital CEOs Ted Garrard, Kevin Goldthorp and Tennys Hansen took time to answer my questions. Thank you. Mark Blumberg and Ken Wyman were generous in their commentary. You guys are great.

The class of 2016 at Humber College, Fundraising & Volunteer Management program, where I sat in for a few days, especially Chantelle Uribe, was sweet and welcoming. Thanks and good luck in everything you are trying to do.

So much research and so many interviews were done for the book. Some of that material is currently resting on the edit room floor, for now anyway. I appreciate everyone I talked to and look forward to continued work on those stories.

My editor Lisa MacDonald took great care of the manuscript and me. Her enthusiasm for the material and contribution to making it understandable to people who may not work in the charitable sector has been great. Designer Kathleen McBride brought everything together so beautifully. Such talent! Jim Hilborn, publisher of Civil Sector Press and a friend for many years, guided *Cap in Hand* through the process in the most gentlemanly way possible. It is a pleasure working with him and his team, especially Mary Singleton who takes care of the day-to-day with much cheerfulness and efficiency. Thanks to Elaine Wong and Kerrie Proulx who read drafts of the manuscript and to Julian Foreman who supplied a chapter title.

To my children, Katie and Evan, always supportive, I say, "we've done it!".

Notes

Preface

Sidney Katz, *The rising wave of runaway wives — Women are liberating themselves: they say to heck with it and leave*, Toronto Star. July, 1973.

A review in the New York Times outlined the plot of *The Burning Bed*, based on a book by Faith McNulty about the real life story of a Minnesota woman, Francine Hughes. http://www.nytimes.com/1984/10/08/arts/tv-review-fawcett-in-burning-bed.html and http://www.people.com/people/archive/article/0,,20088845,00.html

The story of the babies floating down the river is a one I heard about ten years ago. I do not know its origins, but community groups and charities have used the parable since 2008 to illustrate the importance of systemic change as opposed to temporary solutions.

Introduction

Information on the Princess Margaret Cancer Foundation, University of Toronto and UBC capital campaigns can be found on:

- http://www.ibelieveit.ca
- http://boundless.utoronto.ca
- http://www.marketingmag.ca/brands/u-of-t-feels-"boundless"-in-2-billion-fundraising-campaign-40896

- http://news.ubc.ca/2011/09/28/start-an-evolution-ubc-launches-canadas-largest-fundraising-and-alumni-engagement-campaign/
- https://support.ubc.ca/reportongiving/startanevolution-campaign-final-report/

Chapter 1: The Sight of the Forest

There are 33 pages of legislation regulating the production and marketing of maple syrup in Canada. *Maple Syrup Regulations,* Government of Canada. http://laws-lois.justice.gc.ca/eng/regulations/C.R.C.,_c._289/

A common maple syrup grading standard for Canada and the United States was unveiled. Press Release: *Harper Government Strengthens Competitiveness of Canada's Maple Syrup Industry*—Canadian Food Inspection Agency, Ottawa, ON, December 16, 2014. http://news.gc.ca/web/article-en.do?nid=914889. Nancy Greene quotes taken from the same press release.

Canada is responsible for 84% of the world's maple syrup production. https://en.wikipedia.org/wiki/Maple_syrup

The biggest maple syrup heist in history:

- *Global News:* http://globalnews.ca/news/1589998/how-did-18-million-dollars-worth-of-maple-syrup-go-missing-from-a-warehouse-in-quebec/
- *CBC News:* http://www.cbc.ca/news/canada/montreal/maple-syrup-worth-up-to-30m-stolen-in-quebec-1.1266012

The price of a barrel of oil, *2011 Brief: Brent crude oil averages over $100 per barrel in 2011,* U.S. Energy Information Administration, January 12, 2012. http://www.eia.gov/todayinenergy/detail.cfm?id=4550#

Charity's provenance is scriptural. King James Bible, 1 Corinthians 13, Acts 9:36

Seven heavenly virtues. *Psychomachia,* Prudentius, from the early fifth century, https://en.wikipedia.org/wiki/Seven_virtues

In Canada, charities generated $246 billion of revenue from all sources in 2014.

Blumbergs' Snapshot of the Canadian Charity Sector 2014, April 14, 2016.
http://www.globalphilanthropy.ca/blog/blumbergs_snapshot_of_the_canadian_
charity_sector_2014

GDP of Ireland and Pakistan, World Bank GDP Rankings.
http://data.worldbank.org/data-catalog/GDP-ranking-table

Charitable revenue in Canada, the U.S., U.K. and Australia.

- Canada: Canada Revenue Agency data via *The Blumberg Snapshot of the Charitable Sector.* http://www.globalphilanthropy.ca/blog/blumbergs_ snapshot_of_the_canadian_charity_sector_2014
- U.S.: Urban Institute's *The Nonprofit Sector in Brief 2014 and The Nonprofit Sector in Brief 2012.* http://www.urban.org/sites/default/files/ alfresco/publication
- U.K.: Charity Trends. http://www.charitytrends.org
- Australia: *Australian Charities Report 2014.* https://www.acnc.gov. au/ACNC/Pblctns/Rpts/CharityReport2014/ACNC/Publications/ Reports/CharityReport2014.aspx

In Canada, there are 10 pages of legislation regulating the registration of
charities. *Charities Registration (Security Information) Act (S.C. 2001, c. 41, s. 113),*
Government of Canada. http://laws-lois.justice.gc.ca/PDF/C-27.55.pdf

Chapter 2: Following the Money

Mark Blumberg's views were gathered from an interview on February 7 2016,
from his Canadian Charity Boot Camp on April 7 2016 and from intervening
conversation and email. Information and rules on charity filings are as follows:

- Canada: Canada Revenue Agency data via *The Blumberg Snapshot of the Charitable Sector.* http://www.globalphilanthropy.ca/blog/blumbergs_ snapshot_of_the_canadian_charity_sector_2014
- U.S.: Urban Institute's *The Nonprofit Sector in Brief 2014* and *The Nonprofit Sector in Brief 2012.* http://www.urban.org/sites/default/files/ alfresco/publication

- U.K.: Charity Trends. http://www.charitytrends.org
- Australia: *Australian Charities Report 2014.* https://www.acnc.gov.au/ACNC/Pblctns/Rpts/CharityReport2014/ACNC/Publications/Reports/CharityReport2014.aspx

Figure 2.1, *Country Comparison*, sources include:

- Canada Revenue Agency/*Blumberg Snapshot of the Charitable Sector 2014*
- U.K. Charity Commission/Charity Trends
- Internal Revenue Service Business Master Files/U.S. National Center for Charitable Statistics
- Australian Charities and Not-for-Profits Commission/Centre for Social Impact and Social Policy Research Centre

Figure 2.2, *2014 Nonprofit Revenue By Source, Canada ($246 Billion)* sources include:

- Canada Revenue Agency and *Blumberg Snapshot of the Charitable Sector 2014.* http://www.globalphilanthropy.ca/blog/blumbergs_snapshot_of_the_canadian_charity_sector_2014

Description of federal transfer payments. Federal Support to Provinces and Territories, Department of Finance, Government of Canada. https://www.fin.gc.ca/access/fedprov-eng.asp

The pillars of the Canada Health Act. Canada Health Act (R.S.C., 1985, c. C-6), Government of Canada. http://laws-lois.justice.gc.ca/eng/acts/c-6/page-2.html

The story of Elizabeth Taylor's involvement in the AIDS movement and the Commitment to Life event largely come from the timeline of The Elizabeth Taylor AIDS Foundation. http://elizabethtayloraidsfoundation.org

The history of the AIDS project of Los Angeles (APLA) came from information in the history section of the website of the APLA. http://www.apla.org

Charlotte Haley's background came from her Obituary, In Memoriam/Charlotte Haley, Creator of the First (Peach) Breast Cancer Ribbon and from the Breast Cancer Action website. http://www.bcaction.org/2014/06/24/in-memoriam-charlotte-haley-creator-of-the-first-peach-breast-cancer-ribbon/

Information about Estée Lauder and her pink ribbon was from referenced from *Think Before You Pink » History of the Pink Ribbon*. http://thinkbefore youpink.org

Gerald E. Parsons. *Origin of the yellow ribbon — How the Yellow Ribbon Became a National Folk Symbol*, Folklife Center News,1991. Volume XIII, #3, pp. 9-11. https://www.loc.gov/folklife/ribbons/ribbons.html

Impacts of the recession on American charities — Urban Institute's *The Nonprofit Sector in Brief 2014*. http://www.urban.org/sites/default/files/alfresco/ publication

Scottish essayist, Thomas Carlyle, attributed the origin of the term "the fourth estate" to Edmund Burke. Carlyle himself was said to have coined the term "the dismal science" for economics. https://en.wikipedia.org/wiki/Fourth_Estate

Background on Edmund Burke, *Empire and Revolution: The Political Life of Edmund Burke*, Richard Bourke, Princeton University Press, Sept. 8 2015.

Editorial, Trends for 2016, Globe and Mail, December 31, 2015. Quotes from Pablo Eisenberg came from Philanthropy Needs More Reporters Like Those in 'Spotlight,' The Chronicle of Philanthropy, Pablo Eisenberg, February 26, 2016. https://philanthropy.com/article/Opinion-Philanthropy-Needs/235494

Chapter 3: Our Cancer Future

Alan Rickman died 2016, pancreatic cancer. http://www.independent.co.uk/ news/people/alan-rickman-british-actor-died-from-pancreatic-cancer-a6814686.html

David Bowie died 2016, liver cancer. https://www.washingtonpost.com/local/ what-kind-of-cancer-killed-them-obituaries-for-david-bowie-and-others-dont-say/2016/01/21/b4ac24e8-bf9a-11e5-83d4-42e3bceea902_story.html

King Hussein of Jordon died 1999, non-Hodgkin lymphoma. http://www.nytimes. com/1999/02/07/world/king-s-nemesis-is-an-unyielding-cancer.html?_r=0

Cancer is the leading cause of death worldwide. Eight million people died of cancer in 2012. *Fact Sheet No. 297*, International Cancer Agency for Cancer

Research (IARC), World Health Organization, Updated February 2015.
http://www.who.int/mediacentre/factsheets/fs297/en/

The Intelligence Unit authors noted two firsts for the report. One being the first
time "to their knowledge" that "the global economic burden of cancer has been
converted to economic terms" and, two, it was the first time the cancer spending
gap between developed and developing countries was quantified.
Breakaway: The global burden of cancer—challenges and opportunities, A report
from the Economist Intelligence Unit, Sponsored by Livestrong, 2009, p. 14 – 33.
http://graphics.eiu.com/upload/eb/EIU_LIVESTRONG_Global_Cancer_
Burden.pdf

In 2014, the World Health Organization's (WHO's) *World Cancer Report*
estimated the "total annual economic cost of cancer" at USD $1.16 trillion.
The *World Cancer Report 2014*, edited by Bernard W. Stewart and Christopher P.
Wild, published by the International Agency for Research on Cancer (IARC),
p. 578, specified:

> This figure is the sum of the costs of prevention and treatment, plus the
> annual economic value of disability-adjusted life years (DALYs) lost (a
> measure that combines years of life lost due to premature mortality and
> years of healthy life lost due to disability) as a result of cancer.

> The estimate is derived as follows: First, the value of lost productivity due
> to premature death and disability is taken from a study of DALYs for 17
> categories of cancer covering all cancer sites, which produced an estimate
> of US$ 921 billion for 2010 [3,4]. Second, based on another recent study,
> the annual global economic cost of treating new (incident) cancer cases was
> assumed to be US$ 310 billion for 2010 [2,5,6]. Of this, 53% (US$ 163 bil-
> lion) is due to medical costs, and 23% to the time of caregivers and the cost
> of transportation to treatment facilities. The remaining 24% is attributed to
> productivity losses from time in treatment and associated disability; since
> this portion is also covered in the estimate of DALYs, it was not included
> in the summation. Finally, the cost of prevention is assumed to be 7% of
> the cost of treatment. This is a rough estimate that corresponds to the ratio
> of prevention to health spending in Canada [5,7]. Applied to the global
> treatment estimate of US$ 163 billion, the cost of prevention of cancer is
> assumed to be just more than US$ 11.4 billion.

Although impressively high, the figure of US$ 1.16 trillion underestimates the total annual economic cost of cancer, for several reasons. The most important factor is lack of data on the substantial longer-term costs to families and caregivers, which often extend well beyond the first year of treatment. The figure also fails to account for the value that patients and families place on human suffering, which may be far higher than the productivity losses measured by DALYs.

At the same time, the report said, "based on an initial review of the literature, there has never been a comprehensive body of work on the economics of the global cancer burden." Ibid, p. 580.

Some details on the background of Dr. Christine Williams came from an interview she did with *Impress Magazine, Connecting the Dots: Interview with Christine Williams*, Yuriy Baglaenko, June 9, 2014. http://www.immpress magazine.com/connecting-the-dots-an-interview-with-christine-williams/

Christine Williams was interviewed at her office in the Canadian Cancer Society on March 9, 2016.

Kim Badovinac of the Canadian Cancer Research Alliance (CCRA) provided guidance on resources surveying cancer research in Canada, providing reports and answering questions through email and in phone conversations in February and March 2016.

Cancer Quality Control Council of Ontario defines prevalence. http://www.csqi.on.ca/cancer_in_ontario/

Quotes from Dr. Philip Branton. *The Canadian Cancer Research Alliance's Survey Of Government And Voluntary Sector Investment In Cancer Research in 2005*, Canadian Cancer Research Alliance.

Information for Figure 3.1, 3.2 and 3.3 *Cancer Research Investment In Canada*, 2013.

- Canadian Cancer Research Alliance, 2015. http://www.ccra-acrc.ca/index.php/publications-en/investment-reports-annual/item/cancer-research-investment-in-canada-2013
- Canadian Partnership Against Cancer defined. http://www.partnershipagainstcancer.ca/who-we-are/

Interview with Ted Garrard, CEO, Hospital for Sick Children, June 8 2016 at the Foundation offices.

Figure 3.4: Distribution Of 2013 Site-Specific Cancer Research Investment ($288.7m).
Statistics Canada. *Table 103-0550—New cases for of primary cancer (based on the February 2012, CCR tabulation file), by cancer type, age group and sex, Canada, provinces and territories, annual,* CANSIM (database), Statistics Canada. *Table 102-0522—Deaths, by cause, Chapter II: Neoplasms (C00 to D48), age group and sex, Canada, annual (number)*, CANSIM (database). (accessed 2015-07-31), Ellison, LF & Wilkins K. Canadian trends in cancer prevalence. *Health Reports*, Vol. 23, no 1, January 2012, Statistics Canada, Catalogue no. 82-003-XPE.

The modeling suggests that 40% of Canadians will get cancer at some time in their life span. The number of people in Canada walking around with cancer will increase by 71% to 2.2 million people.
Target 2020: A Strategy for Collaborative Action, 2015-2020, Canadian Partnership Against Cancer, pp 11-15 and Statistics Canada, Canadian Cancer Society's Steering Committee on Cancer Statistics. *Canadian Cancer Statistics 2011.* Toronto: Canadian Cancer Society, 2011. p. 5.

The overall five-year cancer survival rate is 63%.
Canadian Cancer Society's Advisory Committee on Cancer Statistics. Canadian Cancer Statistics 2015. Toronto, ON: Canadian Cancer Society; 2015, p 6.

89% of cancers are diagnosed in people over the age of 50. Canadian Cancer Society's Advisory Committee on Cancer Statistics. *Canadian Cancer Statistics 2015.* Toronto, ON: Canadian Cancer Society; 2015, p 29.

The national cancer Act that President Nixon passed in 1971, President Richard Nixon signed the Act in 1971, declaring "war on cancer." Passage of the Act increased federal efforts to fight cancer. It created the National Cancer Program, which is led by the National Cancer Institute (NCI). https://dtp.cancer.gov/timeline/flash/milestones/M4_Nixon.htm

Chapter 4: Let's *Not* Take That Cancer Journey

In Canada close to 9 million people depend on untreated ground water for drinking. *Groundwater Use,* Ministry of Environment and Climate Change, Government of Canada. https://www.ec.gc.ca/eau-water/default.asp?lang=En&n=300688DC-1

Background on Dr. Louise Parker, Atlantic PATH Our Team. http://atlantic-path.ca/aboutus/team.html and Beatrice Hunter Cancer Research Institute. http://bhcri.ca/dr-louise-parker

Dr. Parker was interviewed by phone, March 23, 2016.

Understanding the translation of scientific knowledge about arsenic risk exposure among private well water users in Nova Scotia, Chappells H, Campbell N, Drage J, Fernandez CV, Parker L, Drummer T.J.
US National Library of Medicine National Institutes of Health 2013.
http://www.ncbi.nlm.nih.gov/pubmed/24444512

Background on the Canadian Partnership for Tomorrow Project (CPTP), Interview with Luca Pisterzi, Program Manager in the National Coordination Centre for the CPTP, March 21, 2016.

A mention in the *Guinness World Book of Records, Research project "nails" Guinness World Record: Atlantic PATH owns world's largest collection of toenail clippings.* Faculty of Medicine, Dalhousie, January 2014. http://medicine.dal.ca/news/news/2014/01/27/research_project__nails__guinness_world_record__atlantic_path_owns_world_s_largest_collection_of_toenail_clippings.html

The following charts are based on information contained in Canadian Cancer Research Alliance (2013). *Investment in Cancer Risk and Prevention Research, 2005–2010: A Special Report from the Canadian Cancer Research Alliance's Survey of Government and Voluntary Sector Investment in Cancer Research.* Toronto: CCRA:

- Figure 4.1: Prevention Research As A Portion Of Overall Research, 2005 - 2010 - 9.87%, p 58.
- Figure 4.2: Contaminants In Air, Water And Soil As Portion Of Prevention Research In Canada - 6.47%, p 34.

- Figure 4.3: Occupational Exposures As Portion Of Prevention Research In Canada, 2005 - 2010 (1.29%), p 41.
- Figure 4.4: Alcohol As Portion Of Prevention Research In Canada, 2005 – 2010 (0.33%), p 33.

Tavia Grant, *Asbestos-related cancer costs Canadians billions,* Globe and Mail, June 27, 2016. http://www.theglobeandmail.com/news/national/asbestos-related-cancer-costs-canadians-billions/article30621739/

Background on Dr. Paul Demers, CAREX Canada—Our Team. http://www.carexcanada.ca/en/team/), Occupational Cancer Research Centre http://www.occupationalcancer.ca/userdetails/paul-demers/

Interview with Paul Demers at his office March 14, 2016.

Silent Spring became a rallying cry for the environmental movement that took hold in the 1960s. *How "Silent Spring" Ignited the Environmental Movement,* Eliza Griswold, *New York Times Magazine,* Sept. 21, 2012. http://www.nytimes.com/2012/09/23/magazine/how-silent-spring-ignited-the-environmental-movement.html

There were 23 Principal Investigators (PIs) who were involved in projects focusing on Occupational Exposures over the six years of the study. *Investment in Cancer Risk and Prevention Research, 2005–2010: A Special Report from the Canadian Cancer Research Alliance's Survey of Government and Voluntary Sector Investment in Cancer Research.* Toronto: CCRA, p 59.

Look at the recent glyosphate controversy internationally. *What Do We Really Know About Roundup Weed Killer,* Elizabeth Grossman, *National Geographic,* April 23, 2015. http://news.nationalgeographic.com/2015/04/150422-glyphosate-roundup-herbicide-weeds.html

Alcohol was classified as a Group 1 carcinogen by the International Agency for Research into Cancer. *IARC Monographs On The Evaluation Of Carcinogenic Risks To Humans, Alcohol Drinking,* Volume 44 (1988), International Agency for Research on Cancer, WHO https://monographs.iarc.fr/ENG/Monographs/vol44/mono44.pdf

A study published by Cancer Research UK in 2011 found that alcohol is responsible for about 4% of UK cancers or 12,800 cases per year.

http://www.cancerresearchuk.org/about-cancer/causes-of-cancer/alcohol-and-cancer/alcohol-facts-and-evidence

Over the entire course of six years, seven PIs focused on alcohol in their research. *Investment in Cancer Risk and Prevention Research, 2005–2010: A Special Report from the Canadian Cancer Research Alliance's Survey of Government and Voluntary Sector Investment in Cancer Research.* Toronto: CCRA, p 59.

The IARC study commented that alcohol beverages have a wide variety of functions for "humans." *IARC Monographs On The Evaluation Of Carcinogenic Risks To Humans, Alcohol Drinking,* Volume 44 (1988), International Agency for Research on Cancer, WHO, p 35. https://monographs.iarc.fr/ENG/Monographs/vol44/mono44.pdf

Figure 4.5, *Canadian Market In Alcoholic Drinks, Consumer Trends, Wine, Beer and Spirits in Canada,* Agriculture and Agri-Food Canada, September 2013, p 3. http://www5.agr.gc.ca/resources/prod/Internet-Internet/MISB-DGSIM/ATS-SEA/PDF/6476-eng.pdf

The five cancers associated with alcohol as a risk factor are running at the head of the pack in terms of the predicted increased incidence of cancer in Canada over the next 15 years. Canadian Cancer Society's Advisory Committee on Cancer Statistics. *Canadian Cancer Statistics 2015.* Toronto, ON: Canadian Cancer Society; 2015, pp 24-28. http://www.cancer.ca/~/media/cancer.ca/CW/cancer%20information/cancer%20101/Canadian%20cancer%20statistics/Canadian-Cancer-Statistics-2015-EN.pdf?la=en

Cancer of the esophagus, which killed celebrated writer, Christopher Hitchens in 2011. *In Memoriam: Christopher Hitchens, 1949–2011,* Julie Weiner December, Vanity Fair, December 15, 2011. http://www.vanityfair.com/news/2011/12/In-Memoriam-Christopher-Hitchens-19492011

Figure 4.6, Genetic Susceptibilities As Portion Of Prevention Research In Canada, 2005 – 2010 (18.7%). *Investment in Cancer Risk and Prevention Research, 2005–2010: A Special Report from the Canadian Cancer Research Alliance's Survey of Government and Voluntary Sector Investment in Cancer Research.* Toronto: CCRA p 38.

There were 88 PIs involved in genetic susceptibility research. Ibid, p 59.

The ethical considerations of mapping gene to affect a cancer cure are significant.

- *Ethical issues in predictive genetic testing: a public health perspective*, K G Fulda and K Lykens, U.S National Library of Medicine National Institutes of Health, 2006, Abstract. http://www.ncbi.nlm.nih.gov/pmc/articles/PMC2564466/
- *Review of Ethical Issues in Medical Genetics,* Report of Consultants to WHO Professors D.C. Wertz, J.C. Fletcher, K. Berg, Human Genetics Programme, Management of Noncommunicable Diseases, World Health Organization, 2003. http://www.who.int/genomics/publications/en/ethical_issuesin_medgenetics%20report.pdf

Chapter 5: Tax Incentives: The Downside of Gratitude

If we use the Etihad deal as a base…*Manchester City bank record £400m Sponsorship Deal with Etihad Airways*, Daniel Taylor, *The Guardian*, July 8, 2011. https://www.theguardian.com/football/2011/jul/08/manchester-city-deal-etihad-airways

USD to CAD exchange rate July 2, 2011 0.96125 CAD. http://www.exchange-rates.org/Rate/USD/CAD/7-8-2011

Interview with Ken Wyman in Toronto, February, 11, 2016.

Interview with Mark Blumberg at his office in Toronto, February 17, 2016.

Branding experts say we are in the middle of "global naming rights explosion." Elise Neils, *Ballpark figures: assessing brand value and the benefits of stadium naming rights, World Trademark Review,* December/January 2012, pp 51 – 55. http://brandfinance.com/images/upload/stadiums_article_1.pdf

Biographical Detail Tennys Hanson. http://www.tgwhf.ca/about/board_bios.asp

How do I calculate my charitable tax credits?

- Canada Revenue Agency. http://www.cra-arc.gc.ca/chrts-gvng/dnrs/svngs/clmng1-eng.html

- Charitable donation tax credit calculator.
- Canada Revenue Agency.
  http://www.cra-arc.gc.ca/chrts-gvng/dnrs/svngs/clmng1b2-eng.html
- Stretch Tax FAQ | Imagine Canada.
  http://www.imaginecanada.ca/our-programs/public-policy/
  stretch-campaign/stretch-tax-faq
- 2016 Canadian federal budget and its impact on the nonprofit and
  charitable sector, April 4, 2016.
  http://www.charityinfo.ca/articles/2016-canadian-federal-budget

Canada already has the most generous tax incentives for charitable giving in
the world. *The Philanthropist*, September 19, 2016. http://thephilanthropist.
ca/2016/09/donation-incentives-the-canadian-advantage/

Chapter 6: How Can You Compete With People Who Are Changing the Skyline?

Sick Kids marketing story compiled from:

- Applied Arts Mag - Editorial - Blog - Better Tomorrows, Unpaused.
  http://www.appliedartsmag.com/thebrief_details/?id=17124
- Cannes 2015/ DDB, *JWT win Silver Lions in Health* » strategy.
  http://strategyonline.ca/2015/06/19/cannes-2015-ddb-jwt-pick-up-
  silver-lions-in-health/
- J. Walter Thompson Canada Wins Big at Strategy Agency of the Year
  Awards | J. http://strategyonline.ca/2015/06/19/cannes-2015-ddb-
  jwt-pick-up-silver-lions-in-health/
- Lori Davison—VP Branding Sick Kids.
  https://www.sickkidsfoundation.com/about-us/governance-and-staff/
  senior-management-team
- *Day in the life at SickKids* » strategy.
  http://strategyonline.ca/2014/11/11/a-day-in-the-life-at-sickkids/
- Award-winning communications expert joins University of Toronto in
  newly created role | U of T News.
  https://www.utoronto.ca/news/award-winning-communications-
  expert-joins-university-toronto-newly-created-role
- *Cossette wins SickKids account* » strategy.

http://strategyonline.ca/2015/05/28/cossette-wins-sickkids-account/
- *SickKids unpauses the lives of patients* » strategy. http://strategyonline.ca/2015/11/02/sickkids-unpauses-the-lives-of-patients/
- *SickKids launches biggest campaign in hospital's history* | Marketing Magazine. http://www.marketingmag.ca/advertising/sick-kids-launches-biggest-campaign-in-hospitals-history-129896
- *Ubisoft and SickKids win big at the AToMiC Awards* » strategy. http://strategyonline.ca/2015/05/22/ubisoft-and-sickkids-win-big-at-the-atomic-awards/

Biographical Information Ted Garrard. http://www.sickkidsfoundation.com/about-us/governance-and-staff/our-president#sthash.PTcvJiiz.dpuf

Biographical Information Kevin Goldthorp. http://www.sinaihealthsystem.ca/en/our-leaders/Executive-Vice-Presidents.asp

Sick Kids Board of Directors. http://www.sickkids.ca/AboutSickKids/Directory/People/P/Rose-Patten.htm

Figure 6.1: *Asset Growth from 2006-2015 ($2.21 billion)*. T3010 forms—Canada Revenue Agency

Figure 6.2: *Asset Breakdown Between Hospitals, 2015 ($2.21 billion)*. T3010 forms—Canada Revenue Agency.

Figure 6.3: *Hospital Row Snapshot*. T3010 forms—Canada Revenue Agency.

Figure 6.4: *Compensation Comparison*. T3010 forms—Canada Revenue Agency.

Hospital for Sick Children—Financial Statements March 31, 2015. https://www.sickkids.ca/AboutSickKids/annual-report/64461-sickkids-auditors-financials.pdf

Hospital for Sick Children Foundation—Annual Report March 31, 2015. http://www.sickkidsfoundation.com/annualreport/assets/pdf/SickKids-AnnualReport-2014-15.pdf

Top international Brain Prize awarded to Toronto-based researcher
http://www.mountsinai.on.ca/about_us/news/2016-news/top-brain-prize-
awarded#sthash.JDjUdo8G.dpuf

Federal Election Expenses

- http://www.cbc.ca/news/politics/elections-canada-443-million-1.3436139
- http://www.elections.ca/content.aspx?section=res&dir=rep/
off&document=index&lang=e
- http://www.elections.ca/content.aspx?section=res&dir=rep/off/
sta_2015&document=index&lang=e

Provincial Budgets

- Alberta Fiscal Plan Expense.
http://finance.alberta.ca/publications/budget/budget2016/fiscal-plan-
expense.pdf
- BC 2015 Budget and Fiscal Plan.
http://bcbudget.gov.bc.ca/2015/bfp/2015_budget_and_fiscal_plan.pdf
- Ontario Investing More Than $50 Billion in Health Care.
https://news.ontario.ca/mohltc/en/2016/03/ontario-investing-more-
than-50-billion-in-health-care.html

More than 60% of total health care dollars are being spent on hospitals, drugs
and physician services. https://www.cihi.ca/en/spending-and-health-workforce/
spending/national-health-expenditure-trends/nhex2015-topic4

National Health Expenditure Trends, 1975 to 2015. https://www.cihi.ca/sites/
default/files/document/nhex_key_findings_2015_en.pdf

Peter Gilgan Centre for Research and Learning. http://urbantoronto.ca/
database/projects/peter-gilgan-centre-research-and-learning

Chapter 7: The Next Best Thing

Jeff Holt has stunning photos of the South Sudanese Malakal Refugee Camp
under Portfolios. http://www.jholtvisuals.com

Alex Perry. *George Clooney, South Sudan And How The World's Newest Nation Imploded,* Newsweek, October 2, 2014. http://www.newsweek.com/2014/10/10/george-clooney-south-sudan-how-worlds-newest-nation-imploded-274547.html

Alex Perry. *The Rift: A New Africa Breaks Free.*, Little, Brown, November 2015.

South Sudan: Travel Advice. https://assets.publishing.service.gov.uk/media/52b420d1e5274a0eec000005/FCO_337_-_South_Sudan_Travel_Advice_Ed7.pdf

UNICEF condemns new child abductions by armed group in South Sudan. UNICEF Media Release February 21, 2015. http://www.unicef.org/media/media_80205.html

British aid worker killed in South Sudan, Sam Jones, *The Guardian,* February 18, 2015. http://www.theguardian.com/global-development/2015/feb/18/british-aid-worker-killed-south-sudan-carter-center

UN Humanitarian Air Service (UNHAS). https://www.wfp.org/logistics/aviation/unhas-current-operations

Damian Lilly. *Protection of Civilians sites: a new type of displacement settlement?* Humanitarian Practice Network September 2014. http://odihpn.org/magazine/protection-of-civilians-sites-a-new-type-of-displacement-settlement/

International Organization for Migration (IOM). http://www.iom.int

Magdoline Joseph. *Gov't to release 89 abducted Wau Shilluk children, Eye Radio,* 98.6 FM. http://www.eyeradio.org/govt-release-89-abducted-wau-shilluk-children/

Eye Radio bills themselves as 100% South Sudanese and "your eye on South Sudan." Find them on twitter @EyeRadioJuba or livestream at http://www.eyeradio.org

Katarina Wahlberg. *Food Aid for the Hungry?* Global Policy Forum, January 2008. https://www.globalpolicy.org/world-hunger/46251-food-aid-for-the-hungry.html

MSF hospitals attacked in Afghanistan, Yemen and Syria, *The Aid Security Monthly News Brief,* October 2015.
http://www.insecurityinsight.org/aidindanger/wp-content/uploads/2015/11/The_Aid_Security_Monthly_News_Brief_October_2015.pdf

Chapter 8: Solving The World's Most Wicked Problems

Impact of Dead Aid

Dambisa Moyo. *Dead Aid: Why Aid Is Not Working and How There Is a Better Way for Africa*, Farrar, Straus and Giroux, 2009.

Niall Ferguson. *The Ascent of Money: A Financial History of the World*, Penguin Books, 2009.

Nicholas Kristoff. *How Can We Help the World's Poor?* New York Times Magazine November 2009. http://www.nytimes.com/2009/11/22/books/review/Kristof-t.html

Andrei Shleifer. *Peter Bauer and the Failure of Foreign Aid*, Cato Journal, Vol 29, No. 3 (Fall 2009) Cato Institute pp. 379-390.

William Easterly. *Stop Sending Aid to Dictators*, Time magazine, March 13, 2014. http://time.com/23075/william-easterly-stop-sending-aid-to-dictators/

Virginia Postrel. *The Poverty Puzzle, Sunday Book Review, New York Times*, March 19, 2006. http://www.nytimes.com/2006/03/19/books/review/the-poverty-puzzle.html?_r=0

Forbes List of Billionaires. http://www.forbes.com/profile/peter-gilgan/

Robert Fox interview conducted on the telephone, May 16, 2016.

Bill Gates' attacks on Dr. Dambisa Moyo and Dead Aid. https://www.youtube.com/watch?v=5utDdxveaJc

Claire Provost, Bill Gates and Dambisa Moyo spat obscures the real aid debate, The Guardian, May 31, 2013. http://www.theguardian.com/global-development/poverty-matters/2013/may/31/bill-gates-dambisa-moyo-aid

Munk Debates 2009: Foreign Aid Does More Harm Than Good. The 2009 Munk Debates: "Be it resolved, foreign aid does more harm than good," Dambisa Moyo and Hernando De Soto argue in favour of the motion. Paul Collier and Stephen Lewis argue against the motion. The semi-annual Debates were established in 2008 as a charitable initiative of the Aurea

Foundation co-founders Peter and Melanie Munk. https://www.youtube.com/watch?v=I8hgCeN5EwA

Is Aid Killing Africa? *Dambisa Moyo talks about Dead Aid on ABC* (Australian Broadcasting Corporation) Mar 17, 2009. https://www.youtube.com/watch?v=HIPvlQOCfAQ

Madeleine Bunting. *The road to ruin, The Guardian*, February 2009. https://www.theguardian.com/books/2009/feb/14/aid-africa-dambisa-moyo

World Vision/Barrick Gold

World Vision Canada Financial Statements for Year ended September 30, 2015. http://sites.worldvision.ca/annualreport/downloads/financialstatement-2015.pdf?_ga=1.263840588.170388823.1452113049

World Vision International And Consolidated Affiliates consolidated Statements of Activities Year ended September 30, 2015. http://www.wvi.org/sites/default/files/F_559610_15_WorldVisionInternational_NoSchedules_FS.pdf

Tampax Africa project. http://news.pg.com/press-release/pg-corporate-announcements/tampax-and-always-launch-protecting-futures-program-dedicat http://www.nytimes.com/2007/11/12/giving/12GIRLS.htm

Mining company contributes to northern hospital. http://www.vale.com/canada/en/aboutvale/communities/community-investment/local-support/pages/default.aspx

Marco Chown Oved. *Fool's Gold: The limits of tying aid to mining companies, Toronto Star*, Dec. 15, 2014. https://www.thestar.com/news/world/2014/12/15/fools_gold_the_limits_of_tying_aid_to_mining_companies.html

Donors not feeling good about World Vision's attachment to Barrick Gold. https://www.facebook.com/WorldVisionCan/posts/10151388773631614

Catherine Solyum. *Conflicts surrounding Canadian mines 'a serious problem,' Montreal Gazette*, December 16, 2012. http://www.montrealgazette.com/business/Conflicts+surrounding+Canadian+mines+serious+problem/7711072/story.html

Daniel LeBlanc. *CIDA funds seen to be subsidizing mining firms*, Globe and Mail, January 29, 2012. http://www.theglobeandmail.com/news/politics/cida-funds-seen-to-be-subsidizing-mining-firms/article1360059/

Barrick and CIDA co-funding new World Vision project in Peru, Barrick Beyond Borders, January 15, 2012. http://barrickbeyondborders.com/people/2012/01/barrick-and-cida-co-funding-new-world-vision-project-in-peru/

Rick Arnold. *Peruvians Oppose CIDA's Joint CSR Initiative with Barrick Gold and World Vision*, Mining Watch Canada, March 9, 2012. http://miningwatch.ca/blog/2012/3/9/peruvians-oppose-cida-s-joint-csr-initiative-barrick-gold-and-world-vision

Dave Dean. *75% of the World's Mining Companies Are Based in Canada*, Vice July 2013. http://www.vice.com/en_ca/read/75-of-the-worlds-mining-companies-are-based-in-canada

Haiti and the American Red Cross

Justin Elliott and Laura Sullivan. *How the Red Cross Raised Half a Billion Dollars for Haiti and Built Six Homes*, ProPublica, NPR June 3 2015. https://www.propublica.org/article/how-the-red-cross-raised-half-a-billion-dollars-for-haiti-and-built-6-homes

Laura Sullivan. *In Search Of The Red Cross' $500 Million In Haiti Relief*, NPR, June 3, 2015. http://www.npr.org/2015/06/03/411524156/in-search-of-the-red-cross-500-million-in-haiti-relief

American Red Cross Responds to Latest ProPublica and NPR Coverage, June 13, 2015. http://www.redcross.org/news/press-release/American-Red-Cross-Responds-to-Recent-ProPublica-Report-on-Haiti

Facts about the Red Cross Response in Haiti, American Red Cross. http://www.redcross.org/news/press-release/13-Facts-about-the-Red-Cross-Response-in-Haiti

Confusion over who was in charge, air traffic congestion, and problems with prioritization of flights further complicated early relief work. https://en.wikipedia.org/wiki/2010_Haiti_earthquake

MSF took a similar approach in Haiti. MSF Special Report: *Emergency Response After the Haiti Earthquake: Choices, Obstacles, Activities and Finance,* July, 2010, p. 25. http://www.doctorswithoutborders.org/sites/usa/files/MSF_Emergency-Response-after-the-Haiti-Earthquake_Low.pdf

2011 South Somalian Famine

Figure 8.1: July 19 Map by the FEWS-NET (The Famine Early Warning Systems Network). http://www.fews.net

Somalia 2011 famine was a U.S.-created war crime, says journalist Alex Perry. *The Current with Anna Maria Tremonti,* CBC Radio, Audio January 18, 2016 (Interview included Alex Perry, War Child's Samantha Nutt and Oxfam's Holger Wagner). http://www.cbc.ca/radio/thecurrent/the-current-for-january-18-2016-1.3408273/somalia-2011-famine-was-a-u-s-created-war-crime-says-journalist-alex-perry-1.3408302

Alex Perry. *The Rift: A New Africa Breaks Free,* Little, Brown, 2015.

Dominic Nahr, visit http://dominicnahr.com to see stunning visuals of Somalia and South Sudan

Morten Jerven

Biographical information of Morten Jerven. https://www.sfu.ca/internationalstudies/jerven.html

Morten Jerven. *Poor Numbers: How We Are Misled by African Development Statistics and What to Do About It,* Cornell University Press, 2013. http://www.cornellpress.cornell.edu/book/?GCOI=80140100939320

Angus Deaton. "Nobel Prize Lecture: Measuring and Understanding Behavior, Welfare, and Poverty" Nobelprize.org. Nobel Media AB 2014. Web. 24 Aug 2016. http://www.nobelprize.org/nobel_prizes/economic-sciences/laureates/2015/deaton-lecture.html

Michael Hobbes. *International Development Is Broken. Here Are Two Ways to Fix It, The New Republic,* November 18, 2014. https://newrepublic.com/article/120318/development-ideas-work-pay-results-and-data-analysis

Chapter 9: The Wolf at the Door

Which Canadian charities spent money on foreign activities in 2014 and how much did they spend? Mark Blumberg, globalphilanthropy.ca, March 18, 2016. http://www.globalphilanthropy.ca/images/uploads/Which_Canadian_charities_spent_money_on_foreign_activities_in_2014_and_how_much_did_they_spend.pdf

> *In Canada, approximately $3.2 billion was spent by charities who are international NGOs. Mark Blumberg outlines the calculation process as follows. We recently reviewed the T3010 information for 2014 relating to foreign activities. The database was prepared by the Charities Directorate of CRA in November 2015, and covers about 84,370 charities (97% of Canadian registered charities) and their 2014 T3010 returns. We reviewed the Canadian charities that identified they did foreign activities through funding projects abroad (approximately 5,371 charities identified spending funds abroad of the 5400). We also list which identified they received CIDA funding and how much was spent on those arrangements. The total amount claimed is about $3,166,642,696.00. Keep in mind that additional funds are spent by Canadian charities, for example, when making gifts to "qualified donees" that are prescribed universities or UN agencies and they are not included in this document.*

Givedirectly.org is the brainchild of a small venture-backed, NY-based team. https://www.givedirectly.org/public-coverage

Foster Parents Plan changed its name in 2006 to "better reflect how we work." http://plancanada.ca/fosterparentsplan

Biographical details of Russ Reid

- Ted W. Engstrom, Reflections On A Pilgrimage: Six Decades of Service, Loyal Publishing, Sisters, Oregon, 1999, pp 81- 106. http://www.ccel.us/reflections.toc.html
- Founder of *Russ Reid Dies*, Reid built the largest marketing firm serving nonprofit organizations in North America. https://russreid.com/2013/12/founder-of-russ-reid-dies/

The technique, developed by Greenpeace in Europe, was so successful that many others, especially iNGOs, tried it for themselves. SOFII, *Greenpeace International: the reinvention of face-to-face fundraising*, September 26, 2009. http://sofii.org/case-study/greenpeace-international-the-reinvention-of-face-to-face-fundraising

In the U.K., F2F canvassers started to become known as "chuggers," a combination of the words "charity" and "mugger." http://dictionary.cambridge.org/dictionary/english/chugger

And there's no smaller group of people than the people involved what's called philanthrocapitalism. *The birth of philanthrocapitalism, The Economist magazine*, February 23, 2006. http://www.economist.com/node/5517656

Paul Waldie. *For Canada's charities, this is a time of crisis and a moment of opportunity*, Globe and Mail, October 28, 2011. http://www.theglobeandmail.com/life/giving/for-canadas-charities-this-is-a-time-of-crisis-and-a-moment-of-opportunity/article559719/?page=all

Sue-Lynn Moses. *Coop Dreams: How Bill Gates Plans to Change the World with Chickens*, Inside Philanthropy, June 24, 2016. http://www.insidephilanthropy.com/home/2016/6/24/coop-dreams-how-bill-gates-plans-to-change-the-world-with-ch.html

Michal Addady. *Bolivia Rejects 'Offensive' Chicken Donation From Bill Gates*, Fortune, June 17, 2016. http://fortune.com/2016/06/16/bolivia-bill-gates/

Bill Gates' critique of Dambisa Moyo and Dead Aid, May 2013. https://www.youtube.com/watch?v=5utDdxveaJc

David Rieff. *Philanthrocapitalism: A Self-Love Story, The Nation*, October 1, 2015. https://www.thenation.com/article/philanthrocapitalism-a-self-love-story/

Chapter 10: Don't Mention the "P" Word

"...the art of looking for trouble, finding it everywhere, diagnosing it incorrectly and applying the wrong remedies." - Groucho Marx. https://en.wikiquote.org/wiki/Groucho_Marx

"...democracy is when the indigent, and not the men of property, are the rulers." - Aristotle. https://en.wikiquote.org/wiki/Talk:Aristotle

Public Perceptions of the Ethics of Political Leadership, The Gandalf Group, November 5, 2014. http://www.ryerson.ca/content/dam/trlc/pdf/EPL_Survey.pdf

Charles Dickens. *A Christmas Carol*, Chapman and Hall, 186, Strand, 1843.

A Code of Good Practice on Policy Dialogue: Building on An Accord Between the Government of Canada and the Voluntary Sector, Joint Accord Table of the Voluntary Sector Initiative, October 22, 2002. http://www.vsi-isbc.org/eng/policy/pdf/codes_policy.pdf

The UK Government's Compact. The UK Compact with the voluntary sector was made in November 1998, and renewed in 2010. The Compact, created in partnership with Compact Voice, representing civil society organizations on Compact, HM Government. https://www.gov.uk/government/uploads/system/uploads/attachment_data/file/214617/the_compact.pdf

Blumberg's Canadian Charity Sector Snapshot, 2014. Canada: Canada Revenue Agency data via *The Blumberg Snapshot of the Charitable Sector*. http://www.globalphilanthropy.ca/blog/blumbergs_snapshot_of_the_canadian_charity_sector_2014

The Environics Communications CanTrust Index, Environics Communications, April 22, 2016. http://environicspr.com/ca/about/environics-communications-cantrust-index/

Political activities self-assessment tool, Canada Revenue Agency. http://www.cra-arc.gc.ca/chrts-gvng/chrts/cmmnctn/pltcl-ctvts/slf-ssmnt-tl-eng.html

Political Activities Permitted by Charities, Canada Revenue Agency. http://www.cra-arc.gc.ca/chrts-gvng/chrts/plcy/cps/cps-022-eng.html#14-3

Office of the Commissioner of Lobbying of Canada. https://lobbycanada.gc.ca/app/secure/ocl/lrs/do/clntSmmrySrch?lang=eng

Chapter 11: Distribution Should Undo Excess, and Each Man Have Enough

Vilfredo Pareto (1848-1923), The Concise Encyclopedia of Economics.
http://www.econlib.org/library/Enc/bios/Pareto.html

The national average for high school graduation in Canada is 85%. Table A.2.1:
Upper secondary graduation rates by sex, Canada, provinces and territories, 2011,
Statistics Canada (Modified 2015-11-27.) http://www.statcan.gc.ca/pub/81-
604-x/2014001/t/tbla.2.1-eng.htm

Average Salary in Canada. http://www.livingin-canada.com/work-salaries-
wages-canada.html

Children's Aid Foundation Annual Report 2014/2015. https://www.cafdn.org/
annual-report/

Cancer in Children in Canada (0-14 years)—Public Health Agency of Canada.
http://www.phac-aspc.gc.ca/cd-mc/cancer/fs-fi/cancer-child-enfant/index-eng.php

The Health of Canadian Children—The Chief Public Health Officer's Report
on The State of Public Health in Canada, Public Health Agency of Canada,
Chapter 3, 2009. http://www.phac-aspc.gc.ca/cphorsphc-respcacsp/2009/fr-rc/
cphorsphc-respcacsp06-eng.php

Natalie L Yanchar, Lynne J Warda, Pamela Fuselli. *Child and youth injury
prevention: A public health approach*, Canadian Paediatric Society, November 2
2012. http://www.cps.ca/documents/position/child-and-youth-injury-
prevention

Remarks by the President on Economic Mobility, White House Media Release,
December 04, 2013. https://www.whitehouse.gov/the-press-office/2013/12/04/
remarks-president-economic-mobility

John Cassidy, *Pope Francis's Challenge To Global Capitalism, The New Yorker*,
December 3, 2013. http://www.newyorker.com/news/john-cassidy/
pope-franciss-challenge-to-global-capitalism

Blumbergs' Budget Submission to Standing Committee on Finance. *Increasing
the productivity of the charity and nonprofit sector through greater transparency and
accountability*, Mark Blumberg, January 26, 2016.

http://www.globalphilanthropy.ca/images/uploads/Submission_to_Finance_
Committee_by_Mark_Blumberg_of_Blumberg_Segal_LLP_January_2016_
docx.pdf

S. M. Amadae. *Prisoners of Reason: Game Theory and Neoliberal Political Economy*,
Cambridge University Press, February 2016.

Esperanza Moreno, *Strengthening Civil Society Partnerships: CIDA's Operational
Requirements And The Foundation Of Partnerships*, CCIC Briefing Paper #3,
CCIC Deputy Director, February 2006. http://www.ccic.ca/_files/en/what_we_
do/002_aid_2006-02_paper_3_operational_issues.pdf

Kashechewan children's skin lesions not caused by water: health minister, CBC News,
March 21, 2016. http://www.cbc.ca/news/canada/sudbury/kashechewan-water-
health-skin-rash-update-1.3500631

Chapter 12: First, Do No Harm

Acting on the social determinants of health, Public Health Agency of Canada
(PHAC). http://www.cpha.ca/en/programs/history/achievements.aspx

Renata D'aliesio. *Charity reverses stand on scholarships for children of veterans who
died by suicide, Globe and Mail,* Jun. 24, 2016. http://www.theglobeandmail.com/
news/national/charity-reverses-stand-on-scholarships-for-children-of-veterans-
who-died-by-suicide/article30619289/

Renata D'aliesio. *Left behind, Globe and Mail,* May 4, 2016.
http://www.theglobeandmail.com/news/investigations/investigation-canada-
companyscholorships/article29808916/

Europe, Don't Turn Your Back On Asylum: Take People In, An Open Letter to the
leaders of the EU Member States and EU institutions from Joanne Liu,
International President Médecins Sans Frontières, May 13, 2016.
http://www.msf.org/sites/msf.org/files/open_letter_europe_dont_turn_your_
back_on_asylum_takepeoplein.pdf

*EU States' dangerous approach to migration places asylum in jeopardy worldwide: MSF
to no longer take funds from EU Member States and institutions,* MSF, June 17, 2016.

http://www.msf.org/en/article/20160617-eu-states'-dangerous-approach-migration-places-asylum-jeopardy-worldwide

Caley Ramsay. *Women and children to benefit from historic $54M gift to University of Alberta*, Global News, June 22, 2016. http://globalnews.ca/news/2779622/women-and-children-to-benefit-from-historic-54m-gift-to-university-of-alberta/

Michael Massing. *How to Cover the One Percent*, New York Review of Books, January 14, 2016. Covers the notion of "Intellectual capture." Much of today's mega-philanthropy is aimed at "intellectual capture"—at winning the public over to a particular ideology or viewpoint.
http://www.nybooks.com/articles/2016/01/14/how-to-cover-the-one-percent/

Index

44174578R00142

Made in the USA
Middletown, DE
30 May 2017